ARMS OF DESTRUCTION

RANKING THE WORLD'S BEST LAND WEAPONS OF WORLD WAR II

ROBERT A. SLAYTON

Foreword by Wayne Carson, Major, Ret., USMC

CITADEL PRESS
Kensington Publishing Corp.
www.kensingtonbooks.com

CITADEL PRESS BOOKS are published by

Kensington Publishing Corp.
850 Third Avenue
New York, NY 10022

All Kensington titles, imprints, and distributed lines are available at
special quantity discounts for bulk purchases for sales promotions, pre-
miums, fund-raising, educational, or institutional use. Special book
excerpts or customized printings can also be created to fit specific
needs. For details, write or phone the office of the Kensington special
sales manager: Kensington Publishing Corp., 850 Third Avenue, New
York, NY 10022, attn: Special Sales Department; phone 1-800-221-2647.

CITADEL PRESS and the Citadel logo are Reg. U.S. Pat. & TM Off.

First printing: October 2004

10   9   8   7   6   5   4   3   2   1

Printed in the United States of America

Library of Congress Control Number: 2004106008

ISBN 0-8065-2582-7

To Jim Nau

For all the years of friendship

CONTENTS

PART III   OTHER ARMORED VEHICLES

FOREWORD

Wayne Carson, Major, Ret., USMC

As a retired Marine, I have been involved in and listened to many World War II debates on whose weapons systems are better and why. Many of these have been with and between young officers and NCOs—and, in many cases, the debaters could have used a book like this.

Of course, all writing on the weapons of any war will be reviewed by many experts from specific viewpoints. My own take as a Maintenance Officer is that if the weapons system is out in the field and not in my shop, and the crew can hit and destroy what they are aiming at, it is a good system. Perhaps that sounds a little simple, but it is an opinion held by more then just me.

I also think about criteria that have been used for many years in the Marine Corps: Reliability, Availability, Maintainability, and Survivability. I think Slayton contemplates such terms in this book. He gives each weapon a good fair look regarding its effectiveness, even when he must specify the good, the bad, and in some cases the ugly issues.

One point that I came away with after reading Slayton's book was the degree to which the Germans overdid precision; similarly, the Russians built for combat environment. This means that the Russians usually built the better weapon, one that their people could employ when they needed it most. The United States, for its part, built many systems in huge numbers, proving that mass production can win wars.

All can use this book as a way to see how much progress has been made in the effectiveness of our current weapons systems. As for Second Lieutenants and young Corporals, a book like this will help them find their own answers to debates—ones that will continue to rage, yet, ultimately, can be discussed evenly. I would recommend *Arms of Destruction* to any combat unit as a new way to look at how World War II was won.

INTRODUCTION

THE *BEST* weapons of World War II? Oh boy, am I in trouble now! One of my buddies said that writing a book like this would be the equivalent of picking a fight with everyone who has ever read about, thought about, or developed an opinion about the war. He said that I would probably be receiving hate mail by the barrelful, and that even the postal workers would get mad at me. Even worse, this is just the first volume, on land weapons, with a later book covering planes and ships. So let's establish some ground rules early on.

First, and most important, I think it is fair to state that any weapon that saved *YOUR* life during the war has to be the very best weapon of World War II. If you were in a jam and that hunk of technology worked right—the gun that fired flawlessly and accurately, the tank that brought you home—it is indeed the most wonderful thing humanity ever created, because it saved your keister, which counts more than anything. To you. I do not quibble with any of these judgments.

For everyone else, however, other factors come into play, things like reliability, accuracy, firepower, speed, and availability. The trick to this game, I found, is coming up with good, clear definitions of what the best weapon in each category should look like, and then applying these standards fairly and clearly. And there the argument begins; hopefully one among friends.

I have never perceived this book as a barfight, a nasty affair where people get cut up and punched about. Rather, it is more like an old-fashioned discussion around the cracker barrel. What I am doing is putting in written form the same kind of friendly gab fest that guys still have over beer and soda and pizza, where they compare the weapons of war. It is always mildly competitive, always done with the humor and also the restraint that characterizes friendship, and always ends with everyone right and everyone wrong. I suspect somehow that this has been going on since the dawn of the human race, since the time when a bunch of cavemen got together and started talking about whether a spear or a battle ax worked better in the last hunt or fight. And then they went out and drew a painting of their victory, just as so many artists today capture the weapons and the heroes of war. In the same way, I do not consider myself one of the few experts of some sort in the world on any of these subjects, just someone who has done a lot of reading and thinking about this material and has put his two cents worth into print.

So the point of all this is that the book in front of you is meant to be a *beginning*, and not an end. It is designed to start a discussion (and not a barfight!), not to end one. If I get really lucky, it will initiate a few conversations in a rec room, and that would please me. For above all, this book is meant to be fun.

ACKNOWLEDGMENTS

ANY AUTHOR even vaguely honest is humbled by the debts owed to so many other scholars; research simply reveals the brilliance and hard work of one's predecessors. A few of these works are mentioned in the notes, but my gratitude is extended to the many, many writers whose books I have not only learned from, but also thoroughly enjoyed over the years.

I also have a few very specific thank-yous. Jim Dunnigan gave me good advice when I needed it. Part of the funding for this came from Chapman University's Wang-Fradkin Professorship. Leland Estes, chair of the History Department at Chapman, was always a supporter of the project. At the U.S. Army Ordnance Museum at Aberdeen, Dr. William Atwater (Director) and Ed Heasley (Curator) were the soul of generosity and made possible many of the photos used in this book. They are true heroes, performing yeoman's work with far too few resources. Similarly, Craig Michaelson of the American Society of Military History was always gracious and helpful, and is performing an important service to this country. Ed Rudnicki has been just a font of terrific information and sharp insights about every branch of ordnance; this book is richer, and a deuce of a lot more accurate, because of his help. Wayne Carson taught me more about how tanks and armored vehicles work than I ever thought possible, and is just a great guy. And Jim Nau has been my friend for over a third of a century, accompanying me on many of these journeys.

To put it very, very mildly, I am grateful to all of these individuals. My work, my life, is better for knowing each of them. All errors, on the other hand, are strictly my own doing.

A NOTE ON PHOTOGRAPHS

AMERICA IS in serious danger of losing its heritage of land weapons. A quick glance at the photo credits reveals that many of the weapons shown here are at the U.S. Army Ordnance Museum at Aberdeen, Maryland. This is one of the world's three greatest assemblages of armored fighting vehicles: the only comparable collections are the ones maintained at the Kubinka in Moscow, and by the Imperial War Museum at the Royal Armored Corps' headquarters at Bovington, in the United Kingdom.

Aberdeen's collection may be the best of the three. It contains some pieces that are so rare, they have become the only extant copy in the world.

Sadly, it is terribly underfunded, and in a badly diminished state. This is apparent in the photographs, which show sheets of rust and massive disrepair. Many vehicles are no longer available, and more are being lost constantly. The situation has gone beyond sadness, to a national disgrace.

Heroic curators can do just so much with nonexistent resources. Anyone wishing to help preserve this national treasure should contact the Museum Foundation, listed below, and/or their congressperson.

U.S. Army Ordnance Museum
Building 2601
Aberdeen Boulevard
Aberdeen Proving Ground, MD 21005-5201
www.ordmuseumfound.org

Also listed here is the information for another, remarkable private effort to preserve and display military technology. The American Society of Military History Military Museum in South El Monte, California, has a unique collection of military vehicles on display for the public and should also be supported. It can be contacted at:

American Society of Military History Military Museum
1918 North Rosemead Boulevard
South El Monte, CA 91733
626-442-1776
hometown.aol.com/tankland/museum.htm

PART 1

INFANTRY WEAPONS

1

PISTOLS

WHEN THE U.S. MILITARY went to great trouble to choose a new sidearm in the mid-1980s, most of the rest of the world thought they were wasting their time: the Israeli Defense Force, which is arguably the most battle-hardened army of the last half-century, paid scant attention to the issue, continuing to field an old (designed in 1951) Beretta with only an eight-shot magazine at a time when many automatics packed fifteen rounds.

Others go further, folks who consider the pistol the most useless weapon on the battlefield, an archaic, irrelevant holdover from the past. Picture, for example, a classic World War II combined arms attack, with high-explosive shells ripping large holes in the earth, machine guns spitting high-speed lead at hundreds of rounds a minute, armored vehicles churning up the ground while firing armor-piecing projectiles. Then picture an hysterical soldier running around with a very, very tiny gun in his hand, shooting little pellets that don't go very far or very fast. Captain John Nalis, who fought with the Fourth Infantry Division in Iraq in 2003, wrote that the standard army sidearm "makes a nice decoration, but it is not worth spit in a firefight."[1]

Yet, anyone who has gone into combat knows that when one's life is at stake you take as few chances as possible. Of course, a pistol does not have the stopping power of a rifle, but what if the rifle jams? Or simply runs out of ammunition in the middle of a close-combat situation? Pulling a fresh gun is usually faster than reloading, and these are instances where seconds count for everything.[2] Back in the days of Vietnam, lots of grunts were privately acquiring pistols as backups, and most carried at least one, and sometimes more. One soldier I knew carried four weapons at all times, a rifle and three pistols, the ultimate backup being a tiny .22. Amid choppers and shrapnel, that little peashooter seemed to make no sense, but as the ultimate, last ditch life-saver, it had its rationale for a lot of tough combat troopers. Top gun writer Timothy Mullin observed, "The military handgun is rarely used but when it is needed there is nothing else that will do"; he called the pistol "a tool that can allow a soldier to return home safe rather than to lie dead and forgotten in a faraway land."[3]

Most soldiers who carry pistols, however, do it for a very different reason. These are individuals who use weapons other than rifles (such as pilots or tankers), or the rear echelon troops, who are unlikely to see battle. Nevertheless, they need to carry a weapon, just in case something should happen, even though they do not receive much training with this gun and will probably never use it.

Thus, we are already presenting the outlines of one of the key findings of this book: that there are different best weapons for different kinds of soldiers. It is necessary to separate out the combat arms, guys who really used infantry weapons, from either the troops who used more elaborate weapons (like planes or tanks), or those serving in rear echelon units. While the latter categories—the mass of all the armies in World War II—may have been well trained, they had nowhere near the ground combat skill of those who were constantly being reeducated by hard battle.

As an example, Special Forces veterans I have spoken to vastly preferred the M-14 rifle to the M-16 when fighting in Vietnam, unlike many of the regular grunts. The M-14 was big and awfully heavy for slogging through the jungle, and even worse, it only fired in semi-automatic* for all intents and purposes, in marked contrast to the M-16, which was much lighter and could fire on full auto. But Green Berets—experts who could handle the weight and were trained to fire with deadly single-shot accuracy—liked the M-14's reliability and knock-down power, two areas in which it far surpassed the M-16. Similarly, when I asked the late Charlie Beckwith, founder of Delta Force, what his old unit thought of the new, lighter 9 mm Beretta pistol, he said that Delta did not use it. Instead, they stuck with the .45 automatics that required lots more training but fired a more powerful bullet.

So when we ask what was the best sidearm of World War II, the answer depends on your position in the military. Thus, if you were an infantryman, you preferred a semi-automatic pistol. It was more complex and needed a lot more field maintenance, but it fired faster and easier, and could be reloaded in a fraction of the time a revolver could. And tending to weapons, making sure they were clean and working, was part of the survival routine of every soldier, nothing new.

In this category, there are two candidates for the honor of being the best *combat* handgun of World War II; it is testimony to his genius that they were both largely created by the same man. John Browning (1855–1926) was simply the greatest single inventor in the history of firearms, and was responsible for creating, designing, and improving more of these weapons than anyone else. Most of them masterpieces, by the way. His creations ranged from heavy machine guns and small automatic cannon to shotguns and rifles; in the field of automatic pistols, his designs were so well thought

---

*Semiautomatic technically means that one shot is fired for each pull of the trigger, while automatic fire refers to weapons that fire continuously as long as the trigger is pulled back, such as a machine gun. For pistols only, however, semi-automatic weapons are often referred to as "automatics." Confusing, isn't it!?

out, so popular, that to this day in many parts of Europe, these guns are generically referred to as "Brownings."

The competition for best *combat* sidearm of World War II comes down to two contenders: the Colt Model 1911A1, and the Browning GP, Model Grand Puisaance or Hi-Power, the latter simply a literal translation of the former French term.

The reasoning behind these choices stems from a number of factors. First of all, there was not much competition. Neither the Italians nor the Japanese did much of notice in this field, and the Russians basically fielded a modified version of the Colt. Britain stuck with outdated .38 caliber revolvers, a bad idea given that this meant that the always overburdened supply system now had to carry different rounds for their pistols and submachineguns, an idea avoided by the Germans and Russians, who used the same cartridge for both weapons. In addition, the Brits had a tendency for some reason to do a poor job manufacturing these rounds, thousands of them coming out with deficient or excessive amounts of powder, either of which could damage weapons. Not surprisingly, Commonwealth troops, and especially the commandos, switched to Hi-Powers or Colts as soon as they could swipe them. Germany, on the other hand, had a breakthrough with the Walther P.38, the first double action automatic pistol* designed for combat, but that feature is overwhelmed by those of the two pistols being discussed here. The most legendary gun of them all, the Luger, was actually a problematic combat instrument; while terrific to look at, and one of the finest natural shooters ever designed, it had a firing mecha-

---

*To understand the difference between single and double action pistols, start with the notion that there are two operations necessary to fire a pistol: cocking the hammer and releasing it. In a single action pistol, only *one* of these actions is done by the trigger. Think of a cowboy six-shooter—the gunman manually draws the hammer back with his thumb, then pulls the trigger to fire the pistol. In double action weapons, pulling the trigger actually draws back the hammer and then lets it go—*two* actions from the trigger, although with a much longer and stiffer trigger action.

nism that exposed the gun's innards every time a round was fired. This meant potential disaster if rain, mud, dirt, or anything else that appears in the natural world got inside to jam things up. It just wasn't that reliable.

COLT 1911A1

In contrast, the two guns at the top of this list, the Colt Model 1911A1 and the Browning Hi-Power, were superb. The story of the Colt is fairly familiar to most gun buffs. During the Spanish-American War, the U.S. Army found that the standard .38 caliber revolver did not have enough stopping power to deal with Moro warriors in the Philippines. While that gun could inflict what are euphemistically referred to nowadays as "non-survivable wounds," they could not knock a large fellow down. As a result, Americans suffered wounds and fatalities from spears, swords, and axes as their dying opponents, carried along by sheer body weight and momentum, continued to lunge and thrust, even though they were in their death throes. In response, the U.S. Army decided to choose a new sidearm that would fire a more powerful round.

The first step was determining which cartridge the army should adopt. Starting in 1904, Colonel John Thompson (the inventor of the tommy gun), along with Colonel Louis LaGrande, began an amazing series of tests unlike any done before, and not possible today.

The two officers did not want to simply measure the traditional criteria, like muzzle velocity, bullet weight, or foot pounds of energy. Instead, they conducted tests against sixteen steers, two horses, and ten human cadavers to examine the relative impact of different calibers of bullets. Thompson took on the last, gruesome task himself, aiming at corpses suspended by the neck, and then watching to see which ones swung the most to determine relative impact. Later on the two men, accompanied by a sergeant who was an expert pistol shot, journeyed to the Nelson Morris plant at

Chicago's Union Stockyards, the latter made famous in Upton Sinclair's *The Jungle*. The sergeant fired various rounds at point-blank range into the lung and intestinal areas of steers, to determine which caliber would be most likely to put them down. Out of all of this experimentation emerged the finding that a .45 caliber bullet should be used. After that, the Ordnance Board met and chose a pistol to go with this cartridge. A number of contestants were considered and rejected, including a .45 caliber version of the Luger.[4]

In the end, however, they selected a winner, a design created by John Browning for Colt Firearms. The Model 1911A1 is to this day still one of the finest combat pistols available. It combines a soldier's two best friends, reliability and simplicity, the latter resulting from the fact that there were only three main parts: the slide, the barrel, and the frame. The gun would not work if it was assembled wrong (don't laugh; this was not true for all pistols), nor could the slide be blown off by overpowered ammunition, a potentially painful shortcoming of other designs. It would work no matter what the condition, and in the hands of an expert (the point of this discussion, after all), the .45 automatic is an accurate weapon indeed. During World War II, the U.S. government purchased almost 1.9 million of these lifesavers, with the largest contract going not to founder Colt Firearms, but to Remington-Rand, who made 900,000, compared to Colt's and Ithaca Gun Company's 400,000 apiece. Typical of what the weapon was capable of can be related through an incident on Guadalcanal. Behind the lines, three Japanese sought to assassinate General Archer Vandergrift, who was out in the open and unarmed. As one account puts it, "Sheffield Banta, an utterly unflappable old salt, stopped typing a report long enough to unholster his .45. caliber automatic pistol and plug" them in their tracks. Some reports claimed that a number of German officers were carrying these weapons when captured, high praise indeed.[5]

But Browning could not let a good thing sit still, and soon began to improve on his original model. The genius of the Colt

1911A1 .45 automatic (photo by Ed Heasley,
U.S. Army Ordnance Museum, Aberdeen Proving Ground)

Model 1911A1 was that Browning figured out a way to have high powered cartridges be used in a semi-automatic design. Basically, the idea behind all such pistols is that the recoil power of the cartridge, moving backward, will cause the gun to recock itself, eject the empty case, and strip a new round out of the magazine and into the chamber; in other words, the gun will rearm and reload itself after every firing, rather than having any or all of this be done manually. With a low powered round in a pistol, or a heavier round in a big submachine gun, this is a relatively simple process called blowback, where the recoil force is matched by the weight of the bolt, plus tension from a spring. Put a powerful cartridge in a standard-sized pistol, however, and the force becomes so excessive that the bolt will be driven out of the gun, pushing it and the slide powerfully back into the user's face.[6]

Browning came up with the idea of linking the slide for a few seconds to the extra weight of the barrel, a solid hunk of metal; the combination would then offer much greater resistance to the recoil power of a large cartridge. After moving together a fraction of an inch—just enough to slow down the recoil force—the two would separate, and the slide and bolt would continue to move back at a manageable rate. This was done by means of a swinging link that disengages the two parts at the end of its arc.

Brilliant as it was, however, that link was still a moving part, and moving parts can go bad. So for his new gun, Browning substituted a simple shaped cam, milled into the frame, that the slide would ride over to disengage. Nothing could be more basic.

With Browning's death in 1926, work on the pistol, by now in 9 mm, was taken over by Dieudonne Saive of Fabrique National, the Belgian firearms company. Browning had done much of his work on pistols there, and designer Saive is now credited with coming up with the other great innovation of the Hi-Power: a magazine that held thirteen rounds, but still felt comfortable in an ordinary sized hand. It is hard to imagine how inconceivable that number was at the time, but no pistol of that era, with the exception of extended magazine automatics like the Mauser, carried anything like it.

BROWNING HI-POWER

The Browning Hi-Power first appeared in 1935, and it has many of the same attributes as Browning's other great semi-automatic. Like the Colt, it is simple and reliable, and both just seem to feel "right" in the hand. Picking up either for the first time, but especially the Hi-Power, is almost a shocking experience, in terms of the ease with which it fits into one's grip. After World War II, the Browning became the NATO standard in almost every place except the United States (which, of course, stuck with the Colt 1911A1). The Browning was adopted in over fifty countries and served as the standard pistol for many years for such elite groups as Britain's Special Air Service and the FBI's Hostage Rescue Team.

So there is the toss-up: two similar guns, both designed by the same person, both carrying many of the same attributes, both superb weapons for fighting soldiers. Over and over, men who have bet their lives on these weapons and won say the same thing, that the gun was better than the man who used it.

Browning Hi-Power (photo by Ed Heasley,
U.S. Army Ordnance Museum, Aberdeen Proving Ground)

And that, of course, is the problem. Both of these weapons are beloved, and if you use either one, you swear by it. So, which one is better?

Let me be very clear here: I think they are both superb firearms, and no one has ever gone wrong by training with and using either one of them. Thus, it becomes crucial to state the criteria used: simply put, given the similarities, and setting aside minor factors such as that the Colt is slightly bigger than the Browning, the choice is really between thirteen rounds of 9 mm versus seven of .45 caliber.

On this basis, the Colt wins hands down. Go back to the work done by Colonels Thompson and LaGrande. In the first set of experiments, they discovered that when it came to head shots, the 9 mm and the .45 had roughly similar effects; it did not matter if a large bullet lodged in the skull or if a smaller, faster bullet exited, taking half the cranium with it. But when the bullets struck other kinds of bony matter, significant differences appeared, as the large, slow .45s made much greater fractures than were caused by the faster, smaller 9 mm. This, apparently, was even more noticeable when they watched the cadavers swing, as the .45s, which stayed in the body, made the corpses sway more violently than did the 9 mms, which passed through with proportionately less impact. When they went to the Stockyards, the results were the most dramatic of all: ten 9 mm rounds to lungs and intestines did not cause a steer to fall down, but this did happen after four or five shots from a .45 Colt revolver. On the basis of these results, the officers recommended that the U.S. government adopt a gun firing a .45 caliber cartridge. Their findings, no matter how gruesome the tests they were based on, still seem valid today. The Colt wins, in other words, not because it is a better gun, but because it uses a better cartridge. It is the best combat pistol of World War II.

But not for everyone. The Colt works great for a combat infantryman, but it remains artillery—big, heavy, and hard to control—for anyone who is not thoroughly trained in its use. The bulk of most armies' soldiers, in other words.

These men needed something smaller, lighter, and much simpler. They needed something that had no knobs or levers, no safety to worry about, no slide to pull back. They needed a gun that would never jam, because they would have long forgotten how to clear the problem, if they ever knew. They needed the simplest, most basic firearm possible, one that could infallibly spit out a few rounds when called upon, even if no one had trained with, let alone cleaned the weapon for years. They needed a revolver, in other words.

That's right, a revolver. No combat soldier would prefer these weapons, of course: they lacked automatic fire, took forever to reload, and chambered a scant six rounds. But they really were the right choice for those working far behind the lines, or individuals like pilots who would rarely see ground combat, but still needed some protection. With a revolver you just pull the trigger, and it fires. If a round turns out to be a dud—which would jam an automatic—you merely pull the trigger and another round comes into position as the cylinder rotates. It is the simplest and most basic design of pistol, and will just about always work.

.38 SMITH AND WESSON REVOLVER

The best of these all-purpose guns was the .38 caliber Smith & Wesson Victory revolver, originally called the Military and Police Model, and then the Model 10. Light, solid, reliable, and accurate, soldiers carried these everywhere. The British contracted for as many as they could get, eventually receiving 900,000 in .38 S & W chambering (the Brits called it .380/200), and their troops preferred them to the issue Enfield sixguns, they were that good. They also supplied them lavishly to the resistance movements in Occupied Europe, organizations that needed light, dependable guns. The United States, meanwhile, bought another 257,000, built to handle the slightly more powerful .38 Special round. Brits could get them in 4-, 5-, or 6-inch barrels, while the Americans used models with barrels 2.5 or 4 inches long. The mechanism was pure Smith & Wesson—a little long in the double-action pull, but smooth nevertheless, and made of fine quality materials so that they could last forever with little or no maintenance. Though plainly finished, they were exceptionally well made, and fifty years later, still shoot well.

This is, arguably, the most controversial decision in the book; I hear voices assaulting me, saying things like, "A .38—on a

Smith & Wesson Victory revolver
(Robert Bruce Military Photo Features)

battlefield! The cops don't even use that anymore! Get real!" But the whole point of the argument here is that this weapon should not be too heavy or too powerful, because it is for people who don't want to carry anything, don't know how to use whatever they have, and hopefully will never have to fire it. Thus, a .38 revolver, which is lighter and has low recoil, makes more sense than not only an automatic, but even a big old .45 revolver, descendant of the great cowboy guns, which weighed a ton and kicked hard.

I've already discussed the problems with choosing the .45 automatic for these kinds of troops, but I should explain the reasons for rejecting either the Colt or the S & W .45 revolvers, both of which were issued, and would have supplied real firepower.

The problem is, firepower wasn't as important, comparatively, for people who would probably never use this weapon. OSS agents, for example, were real heroes, but worked undercover and hoped to never have to use a firearm. They used small, light Colt automatics, easily carried and concealed, but, in most cases, firing a small .32 caliber round (7.65 Automatic Colt Pistol). British SOE (Special Operations Executive) spies, in fact, frequently packed .38 S & W revolvers as they prepared to parachute behind enemy lines.

The .45 revolvers, therefore, may have been powerful, but were difficult to use. You need a big hand and long fingers to use them well, especially in double action. Plus, they are awfully heavy: the S & W .45 revolver weighs 2.25 pounds and the Colt version is even heavier, 2.5 pounds. Just by comparison, the M1911A1 .45 automatic weighs 2.43 pounds. The .38 Victory revolver, on the other hand, is only 1 pound, 1 ounce, a much more reasonable weight for an emergencies-only piece of equipment.

In fact, this was really a terrific weapon in its own right. The S & W Model 10 is a nice size—it fits well into most hands and is very controllable. The cops in forces as geographically separated as the New York City Police Department, the Royal Hong Kong Police, Scotland Yard, and the Mounties, all bet on this gun and won. It was accurate too; in 1913, the U.S. Revolver Association was the largest handgun group in the world holding competitions, and twenty of its forty records were held by shooters using Smith and Wessons, most of them Model 10s, albeit in a target version.

Let's put it this way: *Gun Tests*, in my opinion the most honest firearms publication in print today, called the Model 10 "the archetypal double-action revolver." Smith and Wesson, furthermore, has sold more of the Military and Police revolvers and its successors than all the rest of its revolver models, combined. It was a great gun, in other words, if you were not on the front lines, and not bad even if you were. For an awful lot of the fighting personnel of World War II, this really was the best pistol of them all.[7]

2

SUBMACHINE GUNS

FEW PEOPLE OUTSIDE of the military or law enforcement understand what a submachine gun really is; for most individuals, it is something that fires in full automatic and was used by gangsters like Al Capone. They have that last part right, but if full automatic fire is the defining characteristic, why is the AK-47 an assault rifle and not a submachine gun?

To understand what a submachine gun is, therefore, we have to go back and see why they were created and how they were used. This in turn will reveal their identifying characteristics as well.

Our story begins back in the era before and during World War I. At that time, all the major armies used powerful, long range rifle rounds, like the American .30-06, the British .303, the German 7.9 mm and the Russian 7.62 mm. These were capable of accurate fire out to at least 800 to 1,000 yards, and could still deliver a killing blow at a mile and far more. That meant, however, that they all had a hell of a kick, that the recoil forces were nothing to be sneezed at; rifles became long, heavy weapons to absorb some of this impact.

Thus, if you wanted to fire these rounds at full automatic you had to count on several hundred rocking impacts a minute; few, if any, humans could take that kind of punishment if it was delivered through the standard hand-held rifle weighing around nine pounds. So instead, designers who sought the awesome firepower of what would become known as a machine gun (i.e., a gun that fired full-power rifle rounds on full automatic), had to produce a large weapon, and even more, one mounted on a substantial, unwieldy, and very, very solid structure to absorb the shock; the German MG08, a typical machine gun of the World War I era, weighed forty-nine pounds, the tripod another seventy-seven pounds. As a result of this heft, and because the rounds could travel so far, the original structures for machine guns looked more like artillery mounts than anything else, and in the beginning stages that was how machine guns were actually used: like field cannons, set behind the lines on wheeled carriages. By the start of World War I, however, all of the armies had developed relatively simpler tripod mountings (although still massive by later standards), and placed them in the frontline trenches to devastating effect.

That potent round gave the machine gun a lot of killing power, but it also meant the standard service rifle was a heavy, awkward weapon. Trench warfare, however, measured distance in small amounts; often the barricades were only 100 to 200 yards apart, so why have a gun that fired out to a mile? Even more problematic was the situation when a line of soldiers actually entered the enemy's trenches; here the length of the standard rifle became truly an obstacle, making it far too cumbersome for those confined spaces. And most only carried five rounds, when lots of firepower was needed for that brief moment of incredibly closeup, incredibly intense fighting. If they ever made it that far, fighting men battling in the trenches generally preferred pistols, grenades, and even primitive, intimate weapons, like sharpened spades that never ran out of ammunition, never stopped killing.

By 1917, however, the Germans were coming up with some new ideas to break the deadlock on the Western Front, ideas that required new tools. All major armies of that time used direct assaults, lining up their men in straight rows and sending them forward to take enemy positions by sheer force of numbers. Mostly, however, they just died.

The Germans, instead, created the stormtroopers, small bands of infantrymen who would travel light, zig-zagging and making use of all available cover, avoiding obstacles and strong points till they got to key targets. When they reached these goals, however, they had to win fast, using devastating, overwhelming firepower. Hand grenades were an obvious choice, but something more was needed.

The problem was simple: how do you get a gun to fire at full automatic, but still remain manageable for a single soldier to handle without having a shoulder dislocated? Looking around, the Germans found their answer in an idea that the Italians had first employed, but never really exploited. In their Vilar Perosa machine gun, the sons of Rome had created a weapon that was mounted as heavily as any of its counterparts, but instead of firing a rifle round, it fired a much lighter pistol cartridge.

German designers sensed that this was the answer. Pistols are fired from a single hand, without the bracing a large, stocked rifle provides; the cartridges they use, therefore, have to be much smaller than rifle rounds. As a result, however, these cartridges produce minimal recoil; firing them at full automatic in a standard size firearm would pose no problem to the average soldier.[8] True, the bullets do not travel very far, usually 25 to 50 yards for aimed fire, 100 at the most, but this was more than adequate for fighting in a trench; one of the earliest weapons of this sort, the Thompson, was, in fact, referred to in advertisements as a "trench broom," a weapon that would quickly and thoroughly sweep a crevasse of enemy soldiers.

Thus was born the submachine gun, and its definition now becomes clear: it is a stocked firearm, firing at full automatic, using *pistol rounds*. Take away that last criteria (as in the case of assault rifles, which use shortened rifle rounds—see the next section), and you have a different creature altogether, despite an incredible number of mislabelings over the years.

The submachine gun has never had an easy history. Old-fashioned soldiers eschewed them, at first because they felt that a real fighting man still preferred aimed fire at long ranges (they didn't), and later because of the early adoption of these weapons by the American Prohibition-era mobs and by the Irish Republican Army; the British military actually referred to these weapons in *official* documents as "gangster guns" and refused to buy them. That is, until they ran into the firepower of German Schmeissers[9] at the start of World War II, after which they decided they wanted as many as they could get, which meant a lot of catchup, indeed.

Later, after the war, these weapons soon fell out of favor, since the creation of the assault rifle meant there was now a weapon that could do everything a subgun could do, but far better (again, see next section). Only the rise of antiterrorism as a military-police specialty has revived this weapon's fortunes, since a submachine gun remains an excellent tool for intense, close-quarters combat. Beyond these specialized units, however, few line units would carry them, although American tankers packed M-3 Grease Guns in their Abrams tanks as backups during the Persian Gulf War in 1991.

But this abbreviated historic role for the submachine gun meant that its heyday was clearly World War II. Lots of great guns entered firearms folklore, from the American Tommy Gun to the British Sten. Our job is to pick the best.

I want to again divide this into two categories because there really were two approaches to designing and manufacturing submachine guns. One stressed older criteria that relied more on the gunmaker's art; these weapons were beautifully finished, both in their wooden furniture and their metal parts, the latter often milled from blocks of solid steel. Every soldier who carried these weapons cherished them, and ordnance workers marveled at the craftsmanship whenever they had an opportunity to take these wonders apart.

If the first approach could be labeled "craftsmanlike," the second should be called "utilitarian." For the submachine gun was, and remains, one of the simplest weapons of all to make, actually cheaper to produce than a pistol in many cases. It employs the simplest of blowback mechanisms and often features few moving parts. If done crudely, they use lots of metal stampings and can be cranked out in record numbers. Of course, these would not be nearly as accurate as the works of art, but they could be just as reliable. And besides, so what? This was a weapon conceived as a spray gun, not a target weapon, and a cheap, easily manufactured version meant that entire armies could be equipped with handheld, full automatic firepower.

If I had to give a title to this section, therefore, I would call it, "Some Beauties and the Beasts."

THE BEAUTIES

Let's start with the charmers. While there were lots of very good submachine guns in World War II, three of them stand out as truly excellent: the Beretta 1938a, the Suomi, and the Owen.

BERETTA 1938A

Roy Dunlap enlisted in the U.S Army in 1942, by which time he was already an experienced gunsmith; not surprisingly, he wound up in the Ordnance Department. Dunlap served all over Europe and the Pacific, and in his 1948 memoirs, *Ordnance Went Up Front*, he reported that the Beretta Model 1938a was "my favorite gun of its class"; lots of people would agree with him.[10]

The Beretta was, by all accounts, a gorgeous piece of work. Designed by Tullio Marengoni and manufactured by Pietro Beretta, it featured dual triggers for semi- and full-automatic fire, while magazines holding either ten, twenty, or forty rounds were available. The magazines were among the best design ever created, and formed the basis of the magazine designed for the formidable Uzi

Beretta 1938a submachine gun (photo by Ed Heasley,
U.S. Army Ordnance Museum, Aberdeen Proving Ground)

submachine gun in the postwar era. Berettas were always among the best submachine guns made ever, and as a result, reliability for this weapon was way above average; most jams stemmed from poor feeding out of a poorly manufactured magazine, rather than from any other defects. The majority of parts, and especially the receiver, were machined out of block steel, making it very, very accurate.

Above all, the Beretta achieved one of the hardest qualities of all to master, superb balance. Every account says that it was a delight to use, that it handled magnificently; Terry Gander, who writes about small arms for *Jane's*, claimed it was "one of the finest sub-machine gun designs of all time in terms of handling, quality of manufacture, and reliability." Mullin, one of the few modern writers to actually fire all the weapons he talks about, claimed that off-hand or kneeling shots were easy with the Beretta, that the gun was "well-balanced" and "a masterpiece."[11] Dunlap felt it was "as easy to fire and control" as "a .22 . . . a pleasure to shoot," and added, "No one ever bothered with any other kind of submachine gun if he could get hold of a Beretta M38, and keep it. . . . Even the Germans liked it, and they hated to admit anything was good except for their own stuff."

SUOMI

If there was a better gun than the Beretta, it had to be the Suomi. This was the Finnish entry into the submachine gun sweepstakes, and it is considered by many to be the very best of its class; after Dunkirk, when the British decided they really did want submachine guns and felt they should try and equip their troops with the best in the world, they tried to buy Suomis.[12]

The Model 1931 Suomi—that was the year it was adopted by the Finnish armed forces—was designed by Aimo Lahti, who also created that force's pistol, which bears his name. What made the Suomi submachine gun's reputation as the standard for the world was not the design (with one exception); like the Beretta it was a fairly conventional blowback weapon, although with some novel features. The cocking handle, for example, was non-reciprocating; it did not, in other words, move back and forth when the gun fired. You pulled it back at the insertion of a new magazine, and that was that.

That may sound sort of trivial, but it had an awesome consequence. Eliminate the reciprocating bolt handle, and you can eliminate the bolt handle slot, which just happens to be one of the most likely entry points for mud, grit, and anything else that can gum up the works inside. So the gun would naturally be more reliable.

Above all, however, it was the construction that was truly exceptional. Even beyond the Beretta, this gun was made the way Rolls Royce builds cars; only the finest parts, crafted from the best materials, would ever be considered. The Finns used the best Swedish chromium-nickel steel available throughout, then had the barrels drilled, rifled, and lapped by the precision firm Joonas Matarainen, employing the same methods they used to turn out competition target rifles. Solid as a rock, the Suomi is among the most reliable firearms ever made; one modern-day authority reported that it handled more kinds of 9 mm ammunition—both type and brands— than any other submachine gun and still functioned without a jam. Period. It is also one of the few submachine guns that can be bran-

Suomi submachine gun (Sami H. E. Korhonen, www.winterwar.com)

Suomi submachine gun in use (Sami H. E. Korhonen,
www.winterwar.com)

dished as a club, if the need arises, without shattering; it is just
that strong. Well balanced, the gun is smooth and quite controllable, even though it fires at a high rate, 900 rounds per minute
(rpm) compared to the more common 600 rpm. As for accuracy,
100-yard target shooting is no trick (I have seen targets with 50

rounds fired at full automatic, 48 of which are in the smallest or second-smallest center areas), and there are reports from Finland of bull's-eyes at 300 meters. Any that are still around, furthermore, work just fine.

Add to this one of the best designs ever for a magazine. Lahti looked at the drum magazine for the Thompson and then improved on it, producing a seventy-one-round drum that fit so well that, despite its ponderous weight (over five pounds loaded), it did not throw off the gun's balance in the slightest, a remarkable achievement. This magazine was so good that the Russians just flat out copied it for their own submachine guns.

Mullin called the Suomi "dead reliable," and wrote that he preferred it to "almost any other SMG in the world." The other gun, the one he would take over the Suomi, was the Australian Owen.

OWEN

The Owen is arguably a beast and not a beauty, and it most assuredly had a checkered history. It was designed by Evelyn Owen, a rather strange chap to work with. Owen had a problem with discipline and authority, and could not always be counted on to deliver what he promised. Add to that the fact that he was rather a quiet sort, withdrawn and shy—unless he had a bit too much at the hostelry. Then he became a rather wild card, with a predilection for showing up at odd hours, fully armed, no less. One friend wrote about how his "step-brother awoke suddenly to find Evelyn, rocking on his feet, pointing a pistol at him. There was nothing to fear from him, of course, but the initial shock was considerable." Indeed.[13]

But Evelyn Owen also had considerable talent, especially when it came to designing new weapons. Very, very good weapons.

Not that the Australian army was interested. They carried a very strong dose of what many former colonies had, the "if it isn't from Great Britain, it can't be any good" neurosis. Thus, when

Owen first submitted his ideas, they simply told him to submit them to the British Army instead, although no reply could be expected for two years. Later on, when the Australian military had progressed to the stage that they would at least consider a local firearm, they still threw up ridiculous roadblocks, such as requesting that the first prototypes be designed to use the .38 revolver cartridge, a near impossible premise to achieve.[14] Owen eventually got to make some prototypes, in large part because the Minister for the Army, Percy Spender, learned of the project and overruled his generals, forcing them to buy Owen guns and test them.

The Owen looked like no other weapon, then or now, but it all made sense. Its magazine stuck out from the top, instead of having a side or bottom mount like every other such weapon, and

Owen submachine gun (Robert Bruce Military Photo Features)

thus forced the sights to be offset. But this bizarre feature also meant that bullets now were fed into the gun, not just by the power of the spring in the magazine, but also by the pull of gravity, increasing reliability. This also sealed off the insides, by the way; you can drop a bag's worth of dirt into the magazine well, and it just runs out the ejection port in the bottom. Even more important, the gun's cocking handle was separated from the bolt by a bulkhead, which meant that the interior, all the moving parts, was completely sealed and never open to the elements. This held true even when the bolt was being pulled back, or as it punched back and forth as the gun fired in full automatic. This meant that nothing—nothing—could get inside and gum up the works, in marked contrast to just about every other submachine gun, in which the bolt moved back and forth in a long, open slot.

How good did this make the Owen? On September 29, 1941, the Australian army tested the Owen against the American Thompson, and their own favorite, the British Sten.[15] In the last series of events (referred to as "mechanical functioning under adverse conditions"), the three guns were showered with sand as they fired, dropped in salt water and fired, and then given a mud bath and fired. The Sten didn't even do well during normal conditions, and failed completely when dirt entered the picture. The Thompson performed ably as long as it was clean, but could not handle the slightest bit of fouling. And the Owen? It could have cared less, firing through it all without a single whimper, jam, or problem, while achieving "extraordinary feats of accuracy" at the same time. Newsreels of the event show amazed looks on the faces of observers, both civilian and military, especially over the mud test.

In a subsequent event filmed for the news cameras, an operator carrying an Owen walked to the edge of a mud bog, leaned over, and holding the gun sideways with both hands, pushed it under the mud and held it there. Just to be sure the damage was done, he then pulled it out, turned it over, and pushed it back in with the other side down. The thrust was sufficiently powerful that it easily pushed mud into any and every surface.

And then, after that, the incredible finale: the gun was picked out of the mud, and with no adjustment whatsoever, proceeded to fire perfectly. Even more amazingly, the operator then took out the empty magazine (thus permitting mud to ooze into the gun), and inserted a fresh one. Again, the gun fired without a hesitation, just running like clockwork! The newsreel narrator's voice says, "Almost unbelievable, isn't it?" and he's right.

Not surprisingly, the troops loved the Owen, bet their lives on them, and won the gamble. Les Wardman, a sergeant in the 30th Battalion, AIF, said "it was a hard weapon to stop. Sand and mud had little effect. . . . You only needed one failure in a gun and that could be fatal. If you were walking up a New Guinea trail you had enormous confidence if you had an Owen gun with you." Jack Philpott, a sergeant in the Armored Division, echoed this, claiming, "a bit of sand or a bit of mud—nothing—seemed to stop them." Mullin rated it simply as "the best SMG in the world made prior to 1946."[16]

THE ENVELOPE, PLEASE

So which is best among the beauties: the Beretta, the Suomi, or the Owen? I think the Beretta, as superb as it is, still takes runner-up compared to the other two; it just doesn't have the same level of quality, especially regarding reliability. Between the Suomi and the Owen, however, it is a tough call.

Both of these are such excellent weapons, the only way to select one is by factoring out very specific features. Though the Owen was made out of solid metal, it was nowhere near as monolithic as the Suomi, which wins if the criterion is sheer durability. These guns are dependable as mountains and, I suspect, will still be functioning hundreds of years in the future, as long as ammunition is available.

But that comes with a price, and the price is weight. The Suomi weighs 10.3 pounds empty, and a hefty—very hefty—15 pounds with a full drum, which starts to move it into the Browning automatic rifle (BAR) category. The Owen, on the other hand, while hardly a lightweight by today's standards, was only 9.4 pounds empty, and 10.7 pounds with a full thirty-three-round magazine. Based on the simple criterion of what I would want to carry on a long combat patrol, therefore, I would pick the Owen. But it's a close run race.

THE BEASTS

What about the beasts, however? There were lots of them—the British Sten and the American M-3 Grease Gun, for example, but it was the Russian guns that stood out.

PPSH-41 SUBMACHINE GUN

There are plenty of good reasons—*very good reasons*—to argue that the Russian submachine guns were the best of the war. In many ways, the gun that the Soviet infantry used to achieve victory in World War II was the PPSh-41 submachine gun.

Georgy Shpagin, the designer of this gun, had a favorite maxim: "To make something complicated is very simple. But to make it simple is most complicated." Shpagin lived up to his motto, producing one of the most basic weapons ever designed.

The key to the PPSh-41's success was that it reduced weapon design to the bare minimum. One writer referred to this weapon as being agricultural in its simplicity; it had roughly as many moving parts as a plow, in other words, and was just as durable. The mechanism was simple blowback, and to keep the cyclical rate down to a barely manageable 900 rpm, Shpagin simply added a piece of felt to act as a buffer to absorb some of the shock as the bolt slammed back on each firing. Most of the weapon was made out of steel

PPSh-41 submachine gun (photo by Ed Heasley,
U.S. Army Ordnance Museum, Aberdeen Proving Ground)

stamping, even the receiver (the first Soviet small arm to use this technique), and the simple wooden furniture reflected the vastness of Russia's forests.[17] Complicated screwthreading was avoided almost entirely, as everything was just welded or pinned together. The barrel jacket incorporated a primitive compensator into its design (reducing muzzle climb), as opposed to requiring a separate part, but which still improved accuracy over the earlier Model PPD submachine gun by 70 percent. To make sure that even the biggest numbskull in the Russian army could still maintain the weapon, all you had to do to open it was pull a cap at the back, and the entire receiver tipped forward, the gun rotating around a pin in the middle. You could now remove the bolt and spring, and then clean the barrel from the rear. If, however, some poor soldier didn't even want to—or did not know how to—take that much trouble, the barrel was chrome lined to prevent corrosion, a step no other army ever dreamed of taking.[18] Add to this a seventy-one-round magazine copied directly from that of the Finnish Suomi, and you had a gun that fired fast, had an ample ammunition supply, and could never, ever fail, no matter what you did to it, mostly because there was little inside that could go wrong, no matter what conditions it was subjected to.

That suited the Russians just fine. Soviet infantry doctrine was predicated on what they called "an unshakable determination to close with the enemy and destroy him in close combat," and the submachine gun, with enormous close range firepower, was perfect for that. During Stalingrad, for example, Russian squads would travel through the sewers on a 24-7 basis, appearing suddenly behind the German lines. They would fire a magazine from their PPSh-41s and hurl several grenades, causing terrible casualties, then evaporate underground. After that, entire units of the Red Army were equipped with these weapons, up to and including full battalions, something no other army even came close to considering. But it gave these units unprecedented firepower and tactical mobility.

The most famous of these were the masses of *tankvye desant* or "tank riders." Half-a-dozen soldiers or so would be put on the back of a T-34 tank (the later version, T-34/85, actually had handholds welded on), armed with only PPSh-41s and grenades. An endless line of these machines and men would then launch a frontal attack on the German lines, with devastating results to both sides. Average life expectancy of the tank riders—exposed to every kind of fire imaginable—was estimated at three to five days max; they were given that much food and ammunition only, and if they made it that long, they could come back and get more, starting all over again. Those who survived and got to the enemy, however, could lay down a sheet of fire that nothing could withstand, a torrent of lead that destroyed everything in front of it and carried the Russians to victory, but at this horrible cost. The Germans, too, recognized how effective these weapons were, and every report concedes that Wehrmacht soldiers picked up PPSh-41s whenever they could, prizing their opponent's submachine gun over their own because of its huge magazine capacity and above all, its "unstoppable reliability" as one writer put it; neither abuse, nor neglect, nor the harshest of Russian winters daunted this tiger of the battlefield.[19]

Evgeni Bessonov was one of the few tank riders to not only survive, but also to write a memoir. At one point he had picked up

a German submachine gun and was using it in the middle of a
battle; some sand had gotten into the mechanism, however, and
the gun jammed, leaving him defenseless. Just as an enemy soldier
was about to shoot Bessonov, one of his men cut the Nazi down
with a burst from an ever reliable PPSh-41. Afterward, Bessonov
cursed himself, "Why the hell did I carry that German submachine
gun?" and compared it to the "Soviet PPSh submachine gun,
which never jammed in any battle, in any situation."[20]

There is no question that the PPSh-41 was the only submachine gun to *directly* contribute to victory in World War II, making
it the most *important* weapon of its class in the war. Consider the
numbers: only 80,000 Suomis were ever made, and even fewer
Owens, 46,500. Over *5 million* PPSh-41s, however, came off the
lines, causing havoc among the German troops they were eventually turned on. If what counts is the simple, basic ability to deliver
bullets, no matter what, this was the simplest and most basic, and
thus the best.

PPS SUBMACHINE GUN

Except that the Russians didn't think so. Their accounts prefer the
PPS submachine gun, designed by Aleksey Sudaev.

The PPS was a product of the siege of Leningrad, when that city
was cut off from the rest of the nation, and had to design and produce its own weapons from local materials. As a result, simplicity
had to be taken to the total extreme: the muzzle brake, for example, was nothing more than a strip of steel bent into a U and
welded to the front of the barrel, and all the furniture is metal,
including the simple, folding stock. A piece of leather acts as buffer
for the bolt, and finishing work is nonexistent, as most of the guns
went right off the lines into action to meet emergency needs. The
magazine held thirty-five rounds, was as dependable as the seventy-
one-round drum, and the PPS actually featured a better, handier

magazine release than the PPSh-41. And it was just as reliable. In addition, it only required three hours of machine time to construct, compared to seven hours for the PPSh41, and only fourteen pounds of raw steel, compared to thirty pounds for the earlier model, respectively, cutting supplies by more than half, and time by almost two-thirds.

As a result, David Bolotin, in his *Soviet Small-Arms and Ammunition*, claims that "the PPS proved to be the best submachine-gun used during the Second World War." Bolotin cites the fact that its lowered cyclical rate—it fired at 600 rpm—gave it greater accuracy, and even permitted single rounds to be fired by experienced users. It was smaller and lighter as well, important factors to anyone who has to tote around a weapon for endless hours: the PPS with a loaded magazine weighed eight pounds, compared to twelve for a PPSh-41 in similar condition. It was also, by the way, a dream to field strip, far easier, say, than the British Sten. The steel was heavy gauge, and nothing unscrewed, so there were no small parts lying around. Finally, the box magazine was just about the easiest of its kind to load.[21]

The PPS never got the notoriety the PPSh-41 did, the latter being literally the badge of the Soviet infantryman, and featured in endless wartime photos. Some authorities claim that this was because of rivalry between Moscow and Leningrad; as recently as May 2000, the *New York Times* could quote a resident of the latter city to the effect that "[m]any people in Moscow do not like St. Petersburgers. There are strong feelings. There are cultural differences." As a result, some argue, leaders and their publicists in the capital made sure that the product of their rivals never got the attention it deserved.[22]

No one will ever know for sure if this is true, or if the disjuncture simply reflects the fact that only about one-fifth as many PPSs got made as PPSh-41s. One thing, however, is certain. Mullin writes that "[t]he PPS . . . is every bit as good as the finest Thompson . . .

and when you consider the circumstances under which it was designed, made, and then fielded, it is amazing."

Most important of all were the remarks of Mikhail Kalashnikov, a man who knows something about firearms design, to say the least. The legendary inventor of the AK-47 simply felt that the PPS was "the best submachine-gun of the Great Patriotic War. No foreign models could compare with it for simplicity, reliability, endurance, and convenient use."

3

RIFLES

BOLT ACTION

FOR THE TYPICAL INFANTRYMAN, one weapon uniquely defines him—his rifle. No other member of the military carries this firearm in such large numbers, if at all. To the rifleman, however, it is his single most important tool. Uniquely his, it is the weapon he will use to destroy the enemy and defend his life; he will fight, live, and possibly die with a rifle in his hands. And it will be standard issue too: no shortened barrel, no folding stock, no permutations or alterations; just a rifle.

To discuss what was the best rifle in World War II, we have to introduce another one of those guiding concepts, that of generations of weapons. During wartime, military technology moves at a pace unimaginable during the years of peace, as weapons get tested in the most powerful way possible: by finding out whether or not they function in the crucible of war. Data of the most unyielding kind comes in every minute, with the weight of men's lives behind the numbers. New weapons, better weapons are always sought.

This affects the decisions rendered in this book as well. Frequently, the best weapon of 1939 is obsolete by 1945. How can one compare, for example, the standard anti-tank guns at the time

Poland was invaded, all of which were in the 37 to 40 mm range and fully capable of handling the armor of that time, with the Jadgtiger's 128 mm cannon? It seems only fair to break some weapons out by generation, in order to make sense out of our comparisons.

The first generation of rifles in World War II were bolt action affairs. All but one of the major armies of World War II (the United States) began the war with this kind of rifle, and all but two of them (the United States and Germany) ended it with them as well. This made a great deal of sense, as the bolt action is still one of the best rifle designs ever devised and remains the choice on many fields of hunting; most likely, it will continue to do so as long into the future as human beings use rifle cartridges—as opposed to some other, presently undiscovered technology—to kill game. Thus, these guns were generally all of solid, dependable make, rifles like the Russian Mosin-Nagant and the Italian Mannlicher-Carcano and the Japanese Arisaka, to name just a few. But two of their number stand out.

MAUSER RIFLES

The most important bolt-action design ever created was the Mauser system, and the Germans successfully installed this in a remarkable weapon, the Gewehr 98. The hallmarks of this mechanism are reliability and strength: the bolt has several lugs that lock into recesses in the chamber, ensuring a secure hold on the cartridge. Even better, the concept has the potential for almost infinite strength; if you want to handle a tougher, bigger cartridge, just multiply the number of lugs, so that the mechanism can withstand almost any recoil. There is no other rifle mechanism of any sort that can make this claim.

How strong can a Mauser design really get? Peter Kokalis, senior editor of *Small Arms Review*, wrote that the "Mauser action and its direct derivatives are the finest, strongest and most foolproof military bolt-actions ever designed," while Timothy Mullin, in his book on rifles, *Testing the War Weapons*, observed, "You can melt the brass before you blow up an M98."[23] The best answer, however, is simply this: in modern times, over a century after the Model 1898 was first introduced, most of the enormous, kill-an-elephant-or-rhino-with-one-shot hunting rifles use a variation of the Mauser mechanism, including the entire line of Weatherby Magnum rifles, even the awe-inspiring .460. To get an idea of what kind of raw power we are talking about handling, consider this: a factory loaded Weatherby .460 cartridge develops approximately *three times* the energy at the muzzle of a 30.06 round, the high powered round the Americans used in rifles and machine guns in both world wars. And if that's not good enough, Advanced Weapons Technology in Athens, Greece, sells (the weapon is "currently available," according to *Jane's*) a bolt-action sniper rifle for the .50 caliber Browning machine gun round that is simply a scaled-up Mauser 98.

The Mauser fought well throughout World War I, being not only solid but dependable and accurate as well. That last quality perseveres, and is the other reason that the Mauser design is also used for a great many of the most up-to-date bolt-action sniper rifles, the kind used by modern police and special forces teams. That's because it is deadly accurate, an attribute of the World War II version as well. One member of the First Special Service Force—one of America's greatest special ops units—remarked on the captured Mauser sniper rifle he used, "That thing was so deadly. It was a little heavy, but, boy, you just put the crosshairs on anything, and it was done for."[24]

When World War II rolled around, the Germans really couldn't think of much that was wrong with this gun; they tinkered a bit, cutting six inches off the barrel to make it a little handier and adjusting the bolt handle and the sights, but the resulting Model 98k (for *kurz*, or short in German) was basically the same weapon they used at the beginning of the century. A tremendous number of these guns were eventually produced, in various calibers and from

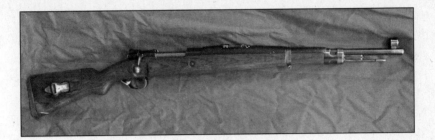

Mauser 98k rifle (photo by Ed Heasley,
U.S. Army Ordnance Museum, Aberdeen Proving Ground)

various nations that licensed the design, and they are still readily available at stores and gun shows. One expert, Ed Rudnicki of the U.S. Government's Picatinny Arsenal, wrote that "[t]he Model 98 Mauser . . . is the most produced military rifle in history, with over 100 million made. The Kalashnikov is getting close, but not quite there yet."[25] In addition, many of the finest hunting and sporting rifles draw on this system. The Winchester 70 series, for example, among the best production rifles in the world, is derived from the Mauser 98k and the Springfield '03, which in turn was an American license-built version of the Mauser. This seems, logically, to be the best bolt-action rifle of the war.

THE IMMORTAL SMLE

Its only competition, in fact, is the British Short Magazine Lee Enfield, often referred to as the SMLE, which some folks pronounce so that it comes out sounding like the word "smelly." From the first this was a controversial weapon: the turn-bolt action created by James Paris Lee, while effective, was not as strong as the Mauser system; no major hunting rifle since the SMLE series has ever been built on this mechanism, for example.

Far, far worse was the length. The British Small Arms Committee that designed this at the start of the twentieth century came up with a radical notion: instead of making a long-barreled rifle for the infantry and a much shorter carbine for the cavalry, why not just create one, all-purpose firearm, a short rifle that everyone could use?

The critics went insane. Compromise, they claimed, was the enemy of excellence, and the Committee had brought in nothing less than an abortion, a mutant that could not deliver long range fire for the infantry, was way too long for the cavalry, and that would fail miserably in combat. One expert wrote in the November 1908 issue of *Arms and Explosives*, "The rifle was always bad, its defects always notorious . . . and the propagation of badness will doubtless continue for several more generations to come." That's powerful stuff; badness, and for generations to come, almost a biblical prophecy![26]

That expert was wrong; so were the rest of them. Dead wrong, too. The gun held up almost miraculously in the endless mud of World War I's Western Front, when precision sniper rifles failed because they couldn't come close to standing conditions like this. The SMLE, meanwhile, built a reputation for reliability that even beat that of the Mauser; Mullin wrote that while the Mauser's action may have been the strongest, "no rifle action is more dependable than the Enfield." Accuracy was also super—at least for the ranges soldiers fought at. Beyond that, who cared? As Ian Hogg, one of the truly great writers on weapons, so beautifully put it, "These are probably very valid arguments if you are trying to put a bullet into a one-inch circle at two miles range, but they lose much of their force when you come down to a four-hundred yard snap shot against a running figure behind a low hedge in the rain." Or, as one observer put it, "most combat shooting standards will be more dependent on 'pucker factor' than the inherent accuracy of the gun." Edward Ezell, curator for the National Firearms Collection at the Smithsonian, also described this reality: when the infantryman "encounters hostile fire, he generally doesn't know where it is coming from or how far away the 'target' is. One often hears after-action reports to the effect: 'We saw no one. We were fighting phantoms.' There are targets out there, but there are only faint clues to their location. Aimed rifle fire is possible only about 15 to 20 percent of the time."[27]

The SMLE's length also made it handy and a much more effective trench weapon than the long rifles of every other country, and it was this feature, in fact, that the Germans copied to create the 98k. Soldiers revered them and refused to use anything else, so almost 3 million wound up being made by not only Great Britain, but other Commonwealth nations as well. Quite a few nations still hold them in reserve, and in the 1980s Russian soldiers, equipped with modern Kalashnikovs, feared the killing power of Afghani tribesmen and their Lee Enfields.[28]

That reluctance of British soldiers to use any other rifle led to some hesitation on their part when the government modified the weapon to increase production during World War II. In truth, not much changed when the British Army switched from the SMLE

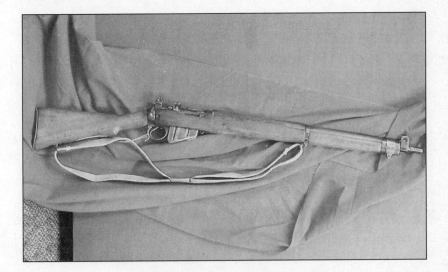

SMLE rifle, No. 4, Mk. 1 (photo by Ed Heasley,
U.S. Army Ordnance Museum, Aberdeen Proving Ground)

No.1 Mark III to the SMLE No. 4: the sights were changed and they got rid of a few inches of wood at the tip of the barrel, but everything important was exactly the same. Nevertheless, the troops took a long time to adjust and accept this weapon; it just wasn't the Mark 3, and that was that.

A DECISION

So which was the better, making it the best bolt action rifle of World War II? The Mauser clearly had a lot more potential and was a more accurate shooter. But the Enfield carried some enormous benefits as well. It held double the number of rounds, ten instead of five on the Mauser, a crucial factor when under fire and reloading means the risk of being disarmed at a telling moment. Far more important, however, was the bolt action itself: the SMLE was far smoother, far easier to manipulate, and most important of all, far quicker to get off aimed fire than the Mauser. If you ever get a chance, go to a gun store that has both and work the bolts on each of these weapons; even dry, even aged, the difference between how easy the Enfield works compared to the Mauser is startling. What kind of impact did this have on the battlefield? The Lee Enfield system of quick turning bolt and extended magazine enabled a trained user to let off an incredible number of rounds, as much as fifteen a minute. At the beginning of World War I, when the Germans were first encountering British infantry at the Battle of Mons, the Brits were able to fire so quickly that the Germans thought they were facing machine guns! Actually, in 1912 the British School of Musketry tested their weapon against the German service Mauser. Using top-of-the-line shooters, they got off twenty-eight rpm with the SMLE, compared to fourteen with the Mauser. And that's from a bolt-action rifle! The top award went to a sergeant-instructor, who managed the astonishing feat of firing thirty-eight *aimed* shots in a minute from a SMLE, all of which went into the inner rings of a four-foot target 275 meters away. That's shooting!

Which was the best? In pure, theoretical terms, it has to be the Mauser. But for anyone fighting in the real world, dealing with enemies at real distances and trying to slog through real mud, the best bolt action rifle ever designed *for combat* is the SMLE.

SEMIAUTOMATIC

Quite a few nations actually experimented with semi-automatic weapons in World War II, but only one nation used this as its primary infantry rifle. The Germans, for example, produced the self-loading Gewehr 41 and its successor, the Gewehr 43. The former was heavy and badly balanced and only 8,000 were made; while the latter did not even start to arrive till late 1943, was primarily employed as a specialist's weapon, especially being distributed to snipers. Russia produced the Model 1938 Tokarev, but it could not withstand the hardships of battle, and though the 1940 model was better, it was considered too complex and thus unreliable, and remained in limited production, issued only to ncos and snipers.

The Americans, however, had a different experience. They had been testing self-loaders since 1918, some of them designed by a fellow named John Garand. On April 12, 1930, however, he received U.S. Patent 1,892,541, covering the system that made the M1 rifle such a winner. Gas tapped from a port at the muzzle pushes back a spring-loaded piston, which in turn works on the bolt, forcing it to rotate out of the locking lugs and move to the rear, ejecting the spent round and recocking the gun, having chambered a fresh round along the way. All very fast, all done mechanically, with no human action, no handle to turn before each shot. On January 9, 1936, the M1 was standardized as the U.S. service rifle, making this the first major army in the world to be issued a self-loader rather than a bolt-action rifle.

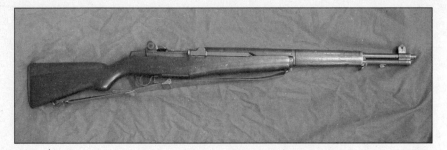

M1 Garand rifle (photo by Ed Heasley,
U.S. Army Ordnance Museum, Aberdeen Proving Ground)

Not that it all went smoothly. There had been a lot of controversy over the ammunition and the magazine. Garand had wanted to use a new .276 cartridge, so that you could have a ten round magazine within the body of the gun, without a projecting magazine. Ordnance rejected that idea, and tried to actually deep-six the entire project on the ridiculous grounds that the new round was inadequate and that if they used the standard cartridge, the magazine would protrude from the stock, clearly—in their minds—an unacceptable state of affairs. A compromise—fueled by the insistence of Army Chief of Staff Douglas MacArthur that this was the gun his men had to have—resulted in an eight round internal magazine using the familiar 30.06 round.

Even after the M1 became standard issue, the old salts balked. At the 1939 National Rifle Matches at Camp Perry, Ohio, the criticisms came fast and furious. This new fangled tool was a freak, not a real combat rifle. No self-loading mechanism could deal with battle conditions; it was just too fragile, especially compared to what the troops had been using since World War I: the Model 1903 Springfield, which employed a licensed Mauser mechanism with its legendary strength and reliability. This new gun would jam at the first sign of rain. As to accuracy, of course, the gadget could not compare to bolt action rifles, and some experts even complained that with a gun like this, soldiers would fire off too much ammunition! Obviously, these were men who had never heard of the doctrine of superior firepower.

A little—only a little—of this criticism was valid. The M1 would never have the accuracy of a good bolt-action weapon, nor was it designed to. But it was no blunderbuss, either, and capable of surprisingly good results in the field.

Beyond that, it proved just how superior a weapon of war it really was. For the first time, there was a semi-automatic rifle that was just as reliable as a bolt action; Belton Cooper, an armored division officer who fought through Northwest Europe, recalled in his memoirs the time a young soldier came up to him with a rusty Garand, covered with mud, that he had found on the battlefield and wanted to turn over to Ordnance. Cooper figured the gun was finished; it had been on the ground for at least two months, he estimated, and was clogged and rusted shut. But just then, he noticed a live round in the chamber and saw that both the bolt and the safety had rusted into firing position. Just to make the gun safe, he held the rifle at arm's length, aimed it at the enemy's lines, and pulled the trigger. The rifle fired like it was brand new, and the ensuing action of the bolt sheared loose the rust and inserted a new round in the chamber. Cooper sent it back to be cleaned and reissued.[29]

Thus, instead of being a disaster, the saga of the M1 is one of overwhelming success. When the Marines invaded Guadacanal, for example, they were armed with Springfield bolt-action rifles (not withstanding decades of efforts by writers—both fiction and non-fiction—and movie makers to equip them with Garands), which the professionals had told them were the superior weapons anyway, more accurate and more reliable. From the first minutes of combat, however, the truth became apparent, that the M1 was just as good. It was actually easier to field strip and maintain than a bolt action rifle, it even kicked less than a Springfield, and above all, could lay down a field of fire like no weapon the Japanese, or for that matter, any other army had at that time. Anyone who had the rare guns had to, according to one account, "keep [them] tied down with wire," and the more that reached the front, the more they were wanted. One Marine corporal in a Raider unit typified this attitude, when he so thoroughly dogged the tracks of a sergeant carrying an M1 that the senior NCO finally had to ask what was going on. "You'll probably get yours on the first burst, Mac," the corporal calmly replied. "Before you hit the ground, I'll throw this damn Springfield away and grab your rifle."[30]

The best testimony, however, came from Marine Corps Lt. Colonel V. H. Krulak, otherwise known as "Brute," a legend of the Pacific war. Asked to provide feedback on small arms to the Ordnance Department, he appeared before the appropriate committee in November 1943.

As was true when Krulak tackled the enemy, he held nothing back. Not exactly a shy flower, he said the BAR was "outmoded," claimed the Thompson submachine gun "does not function well in the jungle," and even felt the .45 automatic round was a poor choice for fighting in places like Guadacanal. Asked about the M1 rifle, however, he answered, "It is magnificent. We will stop there."[31]

ASSAULT RIFLES

Remember back when we were discussing submachine guns and I mentioned that these were not the same things as assault rifles? Well, it is time now to discuss that vastly overused and misunderstood term.

The origins of the assault rifle stem from a series of German studies begun in the 1920s on the future of infantry weapons. German experts discovered what combat soldiers from World War I, from any war, could have told them, that rifle fire is rarely, if ever, directed at targets beyond 400 yards. Later on, in the 1950s, U.S. officials conducted the Salvo studies on infantry combat and came to the same conclusions.

The Germans decided to do something with this knowledge. First of all, they asked one of those questions that is so piercing, so simple, so obvious, that everyone wonders afterward why they didn't think of it. The kind of question, in other words, that smacks of genius and leads to breakthroughs.

The question was this: why use a round that can kill at 1,000, even 2,000 yards, when no soldier shoots at anything nearly that far away?[32] Out of that basic observation, answers and insights came in a flurry. Didn't it make sense, they realized, to produce a new round, one that traveled far greater distances than the pistol bullet of the submachine gun, say out to 400 yards instead of 50 or 100, but still less than what the standard rifle round was capable of in those days? And if they did that, the implications were amazing: the round could weigh a lot less, would kick a lot less, and a soldier could carry a lot more of them. And, it could be fired on *full* automatic, easily and reliably, from a shoulder arm about the same size and weight as a rifle, but with far greater range and stopping power than a submachine gun.

In 1934, the Heereswaffenamt (German Army Ordnance Office) began looking into the development of a mid-range rifle cartridge, and in 1938 issued a contract to the Polte-Werke munitions company in Magdenburg to produce the new round. What they had done was to move from a standard 7.92 x 57 mm Mauser round to a 7.92 x 33 mm cartridge. It had half the propellant of the full-sized round, and the bullet was a little shorter and lighter, even if it was the same diameter. This cartridge, known as the 7.9k (or *kurz*), would enable Germany to produce the first assault rifle in history.

This provides us, by the way, with a clinical definition of what an assault rifle really is. Based on this understanding, an assault rifle is a stocked infantry weapon, capable of full-automatic fire. Most important of all, it uses an intermediate, shortened rifle round that has less range and kick than the full power rounds in bolt action and semiautomatic weapons, but a lot more than the pistol rounds used in submachine guns.

Sturmgewehr 44 assault rifle (photo by Ed Heasley,
U.S. Army Ordnance Museum, Aberdeen Proving Ground)

The story of the new German rifle has passed into legend. Referred to at first as the Maschinenkarabiner42—MKb.42 or machine pistol 42—the name came about because supposedly Adolf Hitler opposed the idea of an intermediate rifle; in order to hide production from him, they provided a name that served more as a disguise than a description. Later on, when he discovered just how good a weapon this was, he bestowed on it a name that has lasted through to the present: Sturmgewehr, or assault rifle.

Whatever it was called, the weapon was excellent, being strong and reliable; one account claimed that it worked despite conditions on the Russian front, and suffered few, if any, stoppages. Its combat debut came in late 1942, and revealed what a rifle like this could do.

German troops attached to Kampfgruppe Scherer, for example, were cut off and trapped behind enemy lines on the Russian front, in the village of Cholm. Alone and encircled, they held on only because of airdrops from the Luftwaffe, and their situation seemed hopeless.

What changed all that was the arrival by air of a new kind of rifle. This gun could deliver a reasonably powerful blow out to all realistic combat ranges, and the Russians had never seen anything like it before. They had expected to face automatic fire close in from submachine guns, but beyond that, figured to worry only about machine guns and bolt action rifles. Instead, they were decimated at long range, so much so that the Germans managed to break out and fight their way back to their own lines.

The Russians never forgot this, or the other times they were on the receiving end of this kind of firepower, and one of the first things they did was to design their own intermediate powered cartridge and a gun to fire it. Though there were some interim models, they eventually settled on a weapon known as the AK-47, which has been produced in greater numbers than any other weapon since the end of the war, estimates of all the variations going as high as 50 to 75 million.

There is no question of what an outstanding weapon the German assault rifle was, and what a pacesetter. In July 2000, *Small Arms Review* carried an article that compared firing the Sturmgewehr 44 to the Kalashnikov AK-47, and the authors concluded that the former was a slightly better shooting gun, easier to bring into position, and easier to acquire targets using standard sights. It also had a softer recoil and was more controllable in full auto fire, although it is unlikely that it would ever match the Kalashnikov's unearthly reliability; you can drop an AK-47 in mud, pull the trigger, and the first round will push the dirt out; the gun just moves on from there.[33]

There is no question that on a one-to-one basis, the Sturmgewehr 44 was the best rifle of World War II. It was a generation ahead of its rivals, arguably better than anything the West fielded, until the introduction of 5.56 mm weapons like the M-16 more than two decades later, and beyond question cleared the way to the future.

But not many were made, and fewer saw combat. Estimates are that approximately 425,000 were built, but only about 100,000 or so ever reached the front lines, mostly on the Russian front; no large unit was ever fully equipped with the Sturmgewehr. The assault rifle remained a promise, rather than a war winner, or as the great weapons writer John Walter put it, "Its influence on post-war thinking was appreciably greater than the contribution to the campaign history of World War II."[34]

So what really was the best rifle of the war? Four million M1 Garands were made, and it equipped the entire U.S. Army and Marine Corps as they fought on fronts in every part of the world. No other nation had a gun that could equip each and every foot soldier with this much firepower. George Patton called it "the greatest battle implement ever devised" and felt that because American soldiers had it, they were the best equipped riflemen in the world. He was right.

4

MACHINE GUNS

THE BEST MACHINE GUN of World War II was one of the more original weapons concepts introduced during that conflict. Its predecessors, the machine guns of the Great War, were divided into two
categories. The main section was what would now be called
medium machine guns, which fired a rifle-caliber cartridge. These
weapons were devastating, heavy pieces of equipment, weighing
as much as 100 pounds when placed on their equally stolid
mounts. Their advantage was that they could fire virtually forever,
never jamming, never overheating as long as their water cooling
jackets were always topped off. During the 1916 Somme offensive,
for example, one section of ten British Vickers machine guns set
what has to have been the greatest extended firing record in history: at the end of that long day of battle, the ten guns had fired
just under 1 million rounds total, without a single stoppage, and
the guns were as ready for action as when the day had started!

Guns like that provided firepower, but not much mobility. In
hopes that the front might finally break open, therefore, both sides
fielded what they called light machine guns, although by later
standards they are still quite a handful. The Germans, for example,
simply took their standard Maxim gun off the tripod, added a
shoulder stock, pistol grip, and a sling to carry the darn thing, then

called the thirty-one-pound contraption a "light" machine gun. The British were only slightly better, with their twenty-six-pound Lewis gun; just by way of comparison, the standard U.S. *medium* machine gun of the Vietnam War, the M60, weighed twenty-two pounds, and its later, more advanced variant, the M60E3, brought this down to nineteen pounds.

A BREAKTHROUGH

After World War I, the Germans took a look at the machine gun situation and came up with both a tactical and technological breakthrough. Simply put, they decided that they wanted the best of all possible worlds. Their machine gun had to be light enough that it could function as a squad automatic weapon, that is, carried in a field assault with an attached bipod, and use smaller magazines (in this case, a seventy-five-round saddle drum). If the unit took to ground, however, their gun had to be capable of being fitted to a heavy tripod and engaging in extended fire. This required a heavy duty firing mechanism, the ability to change barrels in the field, and the use of belted ammunition. In time, it became known as a General Purpose Machine Gun (GPMG), an all purpose weapon, and every army in the world fields some version of this today.

Even more amazing were the tactics the Germans designed around this innovative system. Most armies felt that the basic infantry unit, the squad of roughly ten men, derived its strength, its firepower, from the rifles of its members. In the United States, with its advanced, semi-automatic M1, this became a faith close to Godliness in terms of how devoutly it was believed. The light machine gun, on the other hand, was merely a supporting tool.

The Germans turned that on its head. If each squad could get one of these GP machine guns, the automatic weapon would become, instead, the primary source of the squad's firepower, and the riflemen, the core of every other army's tactics, now became a secondary force, whose primary object was to protect the machine gun that gave the team its battle heft. Throughout the campaigns of Western Europe, the standard German squad, equipped with the best machine gun in World War II (we'll describe it in a minute), felt far superior to the Americans, even though the latter were obviously equipped with a better rifle. To the Germans, that was not what counted.

The first real GP machine gun the Germans fielded was the MG 34, and it was a beauty. It could do everything they wanted, moving from light squad weapon to standard medium machine gun. It was gorgeous and worked quite well. But it could never stand the test of war.

Not because it was unreliable; far from it. The problem, like that of a great deal of German equipment, as will be seen, was that it was much too finely made and took far, far too long to manufacture, using too many pieces of precision equipment. The action, for example, was the most complex ever put into any machine gun, before or since.[35] This was, figuratively speaking, a jeweler's weapon, when a field piece was what was needed. Peter Kokalis called it a "machinst's nightmare" and concluded the MG 34 was "less than ideal."[36]

As early as 1935, Wehrmacht officials were beginning to doubt if the MG 34 could deliver; in truth, they were less worried about the gun than whether or not the five factories that made it could turn out anywhere near the numbers that would be required to fight a major war. So in February 1937 they requested three different companies to come up with alternatives.

The winner of this competition came as a big surprise in the 1930s; today, it would shock few who have seen such weapons as the Sten and the M3 Grease Gun, let alone a Glock pistol. Prior to this time, great guns came from great gunmakers—in the German case, firms like Mauser or Krupp or Rheinmetall. But the winner, Paul Kurt Johannes Grofuss Metall, was a sheet metal manufacturer who turned out lanterns and had never before designed or made a gun. As a result, its engineers knew little of art but a lot about production, and created a weapon that could be turned out in large numbers.[37] Along the way, they created a masterpiece, the best machine gun of World War II.

MG 42

The MG 42 introduced a number of innovative features, including the extensive use of metal stamping to speed production enormously, eliminating expensive machine tooling unless it was an absolute necessity. All over the gun, you could see steel pressings, rivets, pins, castings, and plastic; the old gunmakers may have shed a tear, but all this made the MG 42 a much more dependable gun than its precise, fine-tuned predecessor, and in the depths of the Russian winter, the MG 42 held up far better than the MG 34. Timothy Mullin told how a friend of his linked together 10,000 rounds and fired them in a *single* burst through the modern-day version of the MG 42. This took only seven seconds (that's right— *seven seconds*! Read on for an explanation.) By then, the barrel had gone past red hot to white, and even the receiver was glowing crimson. The owner took out the barrel, put in a fresh one, and fired another 1,000 round set. All without a single problem.[38]

There were other innovations: like the MG 34, the MG 42 could be carried in the assault and fired from a bipod, but was also capable of sustained, tripod-mounted fire out to two miles. A new,

MG 42 machine gun (photo by Ed Heasley,
U.S. Army Ordnance Museum, Aberdeen Proving Ground)

improved—and often copied—belt feed system was introduced as well. It also had the best barrel change system of the war, a device so basic that all it required was the swing of a lever, and the barrel popped out at the breech end; experienced gunners could do it in six seconds or less. This stood in marked contrast to the standard method of barrel changing, which involved screwing and unscrewing a red hot barrel, touchy work even when a wooden handle was attached. Few guns, then or now, have a system this good, and some were even retrogressive; the original M60 machine gun used in Vietnam required American soldiers to unscrew the barrel without any handle, using instead an asbestos oven mitt, an awkward piece of field issue likely to get lost fairly quickly once combat started.

Most important of all, the MG 42 introduced the roller locking breech,[39] an incredibly simple system that later provided the basis for the entire line of Heckler and Koch weapons. This includes their line of MP5 submachine guns, the modern-day standard throughout the world, used by virtually every SWAT and special forces team. The roller block system provided simplicity, efficiency, dependability, and one thing more: combined with the new feed system, this enabled the MG 42 to be controllable, despite the ability to fire at astronomical rates.

Still, how fast is fast? Most machine guns fire at around 600 to 900 rpm, more than enough to keep the enemy's heads down. With these guns you can hear the individual reports, the pocketa-pocketa sound of a Japanese machine gun, or the steady drone of an American Browning .30 caliber.

The MG.42, however, fired at 1,200 rpm. At about 1,000 rpm, the human brain can no longer differentiate individual sounds, so what emerged was a kind of terrible buzz saw noise. Soldiers on the receiving end never forgot it, claiming the MG 42 at full fury sounded like a sheet of cloth tearing; it was just a ripping noise, that was all. To put it as bluntly as possible, it meant that twenty full-power rifle rounds were being fired at you *every second*. That is a frightening experience indeed.

The only weapon to compare with this was a Russian machine gun adopted in 1939, designed by Boris Shpitalniy with the assistance of Irinarkh Komaritskiy (although the finished product was always referred to as the Shpitalniy machine gun). The two men designed a radical new form of feed mechanism, and an action based on a very short stroke piston; the result was a dependable, rifle-cartridge machine gun that had no external power (i.e., like a modern-day Gatling gun), but capable of the off-the-charts speed of 2,000 rpm, although 1,800 is the figure usually given. So on just rate of speed, the Shpitalniy was as good, if not better, than the MG 42.

But the Shpitalniy was never designed as a path-breaking GPMG. In fact, it was an aircraft-mounted machine gun only, and although it was clearly the *best aircraft machine gun* in rifle caliber—and arguably of any caliber of the war—it was never designed as a handy field weapon, and in fact, was never even used by ground troops at all.

While no one knows for sure how many MG 42s were made, estimates range from 400,000 to 750,000, meaning it was fielded en masse to the infantry. This was the best machine gun of World War II, of any kind, and it did its job brilliantly, and still does. Period. In 1957, the rearmed Federal Republic of Germany needed a new machine gun and could not find anything better than its wartime weapon, rechambering it for the standard NATO cartridge, and calling it the MG3. They still use it, and they are not alone. Other nations using the MG3 today include Austria, Chile, Denmark, Norway, Portugal, and the Sudan. In addition, it is built under license for the armies of Greece, Iran, Italy, Pakistan, Spain, and Turkey. Yugoslavia evens builds its own version (the M53) in the original 7.9 chambering. A remarkable record, then and now.

In a recent volume, Terry Gander decided to title his section on the MG 42 not with the name of the gun, but by simply referring to it as "The Ultimate."

LIGHT MACHINE GUNS

One way of understanding how important a breakthrough the GPMG concept was, would be to note that while no one else adopted it during World War II, all major armies did so after that conflict. It was, simply put, a brilliant concept ahead of its time.[40]

The rest of the nations, meanwhile, soldiered on with the idea that they needed both medium and light machine guns, the former heavier, steady, belt-fed weapons, the latter being lighter items that used detachable magazines. Some of the mediums were grand old designs, held over from World War I and still in production; the British Vickers, for example, was a classic that soldiered through both world wars. Others were post-Great War designs, such as the American Browning .30 caliber Model 1919A4 and the Russian Degtyarev DP 1928. All of these were first-rate guns, but none were in the same league as the MG 42.

In light machine guns, however, there was one standout, a gun that is now considered a classic of the twentieth century. It was Great Britain's famous Bren gun.

BREN GUN

Right after World War I, the British army began discussing the need to replace the Lewis light machine gun, a weapon both ponderous

Bren light machine gun (photo by Ed Heasley,
U.S. Army Ordnance Museum, Aberdeen Proving Ground)

to carry (it weighed twenty-six pounds unloaded; that is, without its large forty-seven-round plate steel magazine), and even more so to manufacture, requiring great time and expense to make. Their original notion was to adopt the American's BAR, but of course, they first had to test all available designs.

This began as early as December 1922, but with the pressure of combat removed, trials took a bit longer than they would have a few years before, with a corresponding lack of results. By 1930 no decision had been reached, and a new round of tests was about to begin.

This time, however, there was a new contestant, a Czech gun made by Ceskoslovenska Zbrojovka Akciova Spolecnost of Brno, the ZB 27. The gun was still in the developmental stage and not chambered for the British .303 rifle round, but it had been spotted by the Military Attaché at the British embassy in Prague, and it carried his recommendation.

The tests proved that the attaché knew his weapons; Britain's Small Arms Committee, which had not exactly been a model of enthusiasm in the past, now turned in reports that waxed ecstatic. Minutes included commentary such as, "Functioning—excellent throughout. I doubt whether any other gun has ever passed through so many tests with us, giving so little trouble." It completed not only the usual tests, but even successfully made it through the notorious last stages; the guns were fired, buried hot and begrimed in mud and sand for prolonged periods, given only a cursory cleaning, and then expected to fire a 10,000 round endurance test.

In all fairness, two guns made the cut, the ZB 27 and the Vickers-Berthier (which went on to become a sort of backup for the Bren in British service, and the first line weapon of choice for the Indian Army). Subsequent tests, however, showed that the Czech design was clearly superior; in one subsequent endurance trial, two ZBs had 200,000 rounds apiece fired through them, and the first breakdown did not occur until one of the guns had fired off 140,000 rounds. Later refinements were made at the Royal Small Arms Factory at Enfield, and this eventually led to the naming of the gun, combining BRno and ENfield to create the Bren.

The mechanism of the gun was fairly conventional: gas tapped below the barrel activates a piston, which in turn initiates the firing mechanism. But if the devil is in the details, the Czechs and the Brits made sure that the details on this gun were all the finest possible. The receiver, for example, was milled the old fashioned way, taking a 38.3 pound block of high-grade steel and cutting it down to a finished part that weighed only 4.4 pounds via 270 operations using 550 gauges, each accurate to five-hundredths of an inch. In addition, the company had to use 273 fixtures to hold the item during its journey from bar metal to finished product, during which 18 different inspections were carried out, requiring 740 gauges of various sizes and shapes.[41] The barrel was easily removed via a standard handle, in a manner that was not only quick, but ensured that the hand never touched hot metal; it took only about six seconds to accomplish. One of the most important measures was to include a handy gas regulator, which provided enormous flexibility for adverse conditions; a simple twist, and more gas was fed to the piston, enabling it to overcome just about any natural obstruction such as sand or mud, firing at angles, anything nature or humanity could dream up. Field stripping was among the easiest of any automatic weapon ever made, and the instruction sheet listed only four steps past removing the magazine and making sure the chamber was empty (Ian Hogg said the Bren was one of the easiest machine guns to master). Any stoppages usually came from the magazine, which was made out of cheap metal; the standard, successful response was to give it a walloping thump, turn the gas gauge, or both. Nothing more was needed. Beyond that, the Bren was considered in some quarters to be just a bit heavy for a light machine gun, at 22.3 pounds unloaded.

Bren gunners never worried about this during World War II,

however; quite the contrary, they cherished the things. In one account, a five-foot, three-inch Bren gunner in the Far East— a place where climate sapped energy faster than most places on earth—refused to let anyone else shoulder his weapon, even his No. 2. Eventually, the left side of the gun became polished to a fine sheen by rubbing against his body on long marches, but when they told him it needed to be taken back to be reblued, the soldier went insane with rage, and flatly refused to turn it over. The army, he told them rather vigorously, could bloody well have that Bren when he was done with it, but they had better keep off of it till then.

The man was no fool, either. Because of its design and the incredible effort that went into making it, the Bren had a reputation of reliability, the soldier's best friend, that has been referred to as "legendary."[42] The gas regulator solved most problems, and the sheer quality of manufacture took care of the rest; red hot barrels, for example, got taken off and dunked in streams, and when reattached proved capable of accurate fire.

Speaking of accuracy, the gun was a wonder in that area as well.[43] A reasonably experienced soldier could put an entire magazine into the bullseye of a target at 600 yards, and deliver fairly precise fire at 800 and even 1,000 yards. And while doing that kind of work, the ground slogger could also appreciate the fact that a buffer mechanism, designed in from the start, reduced recoil dramatically, so that the shove against shoulder was substantially less than that from the SMLE, which fired the same round.

The British made 220,000 at Enfield, plus another 416,000 at other sites. It is still in use today, rechambered to take the standard NATO 7.62 cartridge. Every firearms writer states that it is the best light machine gun of World War II and its generation, but Roger Ford put it best, "The Bren gun was a paragon in the true sense of the word: a standard against which all others would be judged."[44]

HEAVY MACHINE GUNS

Only two nations, the United States and the Soviet Union,[45] felt they needed to make a heavy machine gun, one that fired a round way beyond the standard rifle cartridge, in any numbers. Despite the lack of competition, one of these turned out to be a real winner; it didn't hurt that the inventor was John Browning.

A man ahead of his time in most things dealing with guns, by July 1917 Browning was looking into the idea of taking his .30 caliber Model 1917 machine gun and redoing it in larger form for a bigger cartridge. Soon this interest was given official impetus when General John Pershing noticed the trend among European armies to develop larger automatic weapons to use against armored vehicles. He asked for an American version of guns such as the French 11 mm Hotchkiss, an example of which had already been sent back to the United States for testing.

The traditional version of how the .50 caliber round got developed goes like this: at this time the Winchester Company (which, along with Colt, had been working with Browning on this project), got a hold of a new German antitank round. Designed by Mauser, this was a scaled up version of their standard 7.92 cartridge, but much more powerful than the American attempt; this 13 x 92 mm cartridge had a 62.5 gram steel-core bullet leaving the muzzle at 838 meters per second and could penetrate 22 mm of armor at 100 meters.

Somehow, a batch of these rounds made their way from Germany to Winchester after the war; the number was small—less than 100—and no one is sure how they got there or in how many batches, but they provided the basis for what would become the standard .50 caliber round, the 12.7 x 99 mm cartridge.

There's only one problem with this story (which is widely used), and that is the ending. The Ordnance Department actually rejected this design in large part because it was semi-rimmed, which would impair easy feeding in automatic weapons. The gun gurus went back to a formula they knew well, and scaled up the rimless .30-06 round to create what is still the standard heavy machine gun cartridge in use today.

Browning, meanwhile had modified his gun in a number of ways, including adding an oil-filled buffer mechanism that would reduce firing rate in the ground weapons to a manageable 500 rpm; that is slow enough that experienced gunners can fire single shots with some accuracy. Other improvements followed, including the development of a universal receiver for different variations and mounts, and the addition of a heavy barrel to prevent overheating. By the late 1930s, the U.S. Army was starting to procure large numbers of what would be known as the M2HB (for heavy barrel) .50 caliber machine gun.

M2HB MACHINE GUN

It was a war winner, becoming the standard weapon of American fighters, a common sight in airplanes, on seagoing vessels, and in constant use by land forces, equipping tanks, trucks, half-tracks, even tripod mounts, any and every way the GIs could use

M2HB .50 caliber machine gun (photo by Ed Heasley,
U.S. Army Ordnance Museum, Aberdeen Proving Ground)

them. Belton Cooper wrote how, "the Germans had no weapon comparable. . . . If this massive slug penetrated the torso, the hydraulic shock would generate a virtual explosion within the body. If an arm or a leg was struck, the entire limb might be severed. The Germans were terrified of it." Gene Gangarosa Jr., a renowned weapons writer, observed, "this is a weapon that can win battles and perform fearsome execution on those unfortunate enough to be struck by its powerful projectiles." John Irwin, a tanker whose memoir is entitled *Another River, Another Town,* claimed that "the American .50-caliber machine gun was high on the list of very effective small arms in this war. It was the envy of the German Army and the pride of the GIs."[46]

Arguably the best version ever used in World War II was the M16, with four .50 caliber M2HBs on an electronically driven Maxson mount. About 10,000 of these were built, most of them on the free-standing M51 trailer, but over 1,700 went onto the backs of half-tracks, creating a devastating mobile weapon. These Multiple Gun Motor Carriages were originally designed to provide antiaircraft protection to ground troops, but soldiers soon discovered that their effect on enemy infantry was astounding; no one and nothing could stand up to the hail of fire that four Browning fifties could deliver. Years later, at Dienbienphu in Vietnam, some of the last strongpoints to be overcome in that doomed fortress were the Maxson mounts, which seemingly no human wave of Viet Cong could overcome.

After the war, the M2HB became the closest anything has ever come to being a universal weapon. Three million have been made, according to *Jane's* (which also noted, "they never wear out"), and there is not a country outside the former communist bloc that does not have some in its inventory. Over the decades a lot of different companies have tried to come up with something better, and while improvements have been made, especially in barrel changing, no one has ever come up with a replacement, so versions of John Browning's big gun still come off the assembly lines in the twenty-first century. John Walter wrote, in a book published in the new millenium, that the .50 caliber "remains the machine-gun against which all new weapons are measured."[47]

But was it the best heavy machine gun of the war? In the Soviet Union, Mikhail Berezin developed the UBS (for universal Berezin machine gun, synchronized) that was, if anything, even more reliable than the Browning. Tests showed that in aircraft, it worked flawlessly at heights up to 9,000 meters, in temperatures of minus 48 degrees Celsius, and in all manner of maneuvers. In addition, it weighed only 47 pounds compared to the Browning's 64 pounds, and fired 1,050 rpm, far faster than the Browning did in World War II, although in all fairness a late-war M3 version got up to 1,200 rpm. Even though the Soviets made 125,000 of these guns during the war, they were used exclusively for airplanes. Almost none were ever used by the ground forces, which is still true today.[48]

So what was the very best? Once again, the Russians produced the best aircraft gun in this caliber. But for overall use, the Browning M2HB, widely distributed and in land combat all through the conflict and in every possible theater, was flawless and unbreakable. It is still going strong in every part of the earth, and remains the best heavy machine gun around.

5

MORTARS

THE TERM "MORTAR" is actually an old artilleryman's definition, signifying ordnance that fires at angles of between 45 and 90 degrees, different from a gun (0 to 45 degrees) or a howitzer (0 to 90 degrees elevation). During the Civil War, for example, there were plenty of examples of mortars about, short, stocky, heavy artillery weapons that fired shells at the proper elevation.

All that changed during World War I, when the modern mortar was invented. Troops needed a small, light, compact weapon that could lob shells at a high angle into the opposing trench. In 1915, Sir Wilfred Stokes of the British Army began development of a design later refined by the Brandt Company in France during the 1920s and 1930s, and would hold for all similar weapons to follow. This consisted of a smoothbore tube, sealed at the bottom and resting on a base plate, supported by a bipod, and with some kind of elevating apparatus for aiming. The shell was a teardrop shaped projectile with fins, the propellant in the long tube at the bottom, with extra force coming from rings of smokeless powder attached at the base. A gunner simply dropped this down the chute; at the bottom it struck a firing pin in the base of the tube, setting off the charges, and flinging the projectile toward the enemy's lines.

The basic soundness of this design, which persists virtually unchanged to the present day, meant that most of the mortars of World War II were fairly comparable. Take a look for example, at the figures for a few of the standard mortars used by three different nations during the war, and notice how similar they are:

Country	Caliber	Weight	Projectile	Range
United States	81 mm	136 lbs	6.9 lbs	2,560 yds
Soviet Union	82 mm	99 lbs	7.4 lbs	3,100 yds
Germany	81 mm	125 lbs	7.5 lbs	2,625 yds

Thus, it is hard to find one mortar that excelled in World War II, but it is there: the Russians made it, and it was in 120 mm.

RUSSIAN 120 MM MORTAR

As a general rule, the Russians used mortars more extensively than any other combatant in the war. They are easy and cheap to make, as is their ammunition, relative to an artillery piece, and they can deliver a lot more firepower a lot faster than a comparable battery of heavy, rifled weapons. Even more important to a Russian army painfully short of modern communication networks, it was a much more localized system, under the control of local officers and much easier to command than a system of farflung artillery batteries requiring a complex communication net. The Russians went all out with mortars, using them at every operational stage through the battalion, regiment, and even the division level. During the war, they produced 348,000 mortars of various calibers, more than the total of all other nations *combined*, even including the industrial powerhouse of the United States.

Not that this story was always rosy. This also meant a top-heavy organization, where authority rested at higher echelons; most armies considered the mortar an infantry weapon, attaching it to companies or battalions. The Russians, on the other hand, often assigned them to the artillery sections that fought with larger units, and this meant less flexibility than their Western counterparts.

But if there were impediments when it came to tactical doctrine, there was no such question when it came to the Russian mortars' efficiency and firepower. In particular, they specialized in one weapon that no one else paid much attention to, the 120 mm mortar.

The Russians were, in fact, the first nation to introduce a weapon in this large caliber, and their version was outstanding. Introduced in 1938, it was conventional in design, but a perfect balance between firepower, mobility, and range. Capable of firing a 35-pound high explosive shell at a rate of ten a minute, a four gun battery was an awesome sight to behold.

German soldiers certainly thought so. They had nothing to compare to this at first, and its salvos devastated their ranks; when the Russians brought in the even more powerful 160 mm mortars (the largest mortar in general use during the war), their enemies thought they were under air attack, it felt so much like heavy bombs were being dropped on them.

Russian 120 mm mortar (photo by author,
U.S. Army Ordnance Museum, Aberdeen Proving Ground)

It was not just the shell, however, it was the weapon itself, and how it was used. German doctrine was supreme when it came to lighter mortars, but they felt the larger ones had little place on the battlefield, too big to be an infantry weapon but not as useful as a piece of artillery.

That is, until the Germans met up with the Russian 120 mm. They used every one they could capture, and then paid the ultimate compliment, especially to an enemy they considered racially inferior, manufacturing an exact copy. They duplicated the Russian version in every detail, except for a few parts in the aiming mechanism.

No other nation perceived and used this caliber mortar in anywhere near the same numbers. The Americans, for example, fielded a 105 mm mortar, but restricted its use primarily to chemical warfare, and as a result it mostly just laid down smoke screens. Russian ordnance officers, on the other hand, recognized that their heavy mortar fired a round as large as the 122 mm howitzers to a range half as far, but at *three* times the rate of fire. And it weighed only one-fifth as much as the howitzer to boot!

One authority said the Russian 120 mm mortar "may have been the most efficient indirect fire piece of the war," and a good case could be made that he was right. The Russians never found a reason to make anything different, and it still sits in every former Soviet bloc armory, ready to go, while the Chinese are offering their copy for the export market, even in a new century. Ian Hogg wrote that, "[t]he best German mortar of the war was, in fact, not German; it was Russian," and adds, "it is probably fair to say that it was the best mortar of the war." Who are we to disagree?[49]

6

ANTI-TANK WEAPONS

THE INVENTION of an effective infantry anti-tank weapon in World War II owed its success to two developments, one fairly obvious to understand, the other much less so.

As early as 1918, the American scientist Robert Goddard had developed a small rocket launcher that could deliver a minimal payload, but the idea was rejected until Leslie Skinner came along. Fascinated by rockets since his teens, Skinner had meanwhile gone to West Point and was commissioned in 1924. From then until 1940, he worked on and off on a variety of rocket projects—many of them involving weapons fired from planes, and not by ground troops—but none of them were looked on with all that much enthusiasm by his superiors.

But war in Europe, and especially the blitzkrieg with its massed use of tanks, changed that overnight. In November 1940, Skinner found himself assigned to the project that had seemingly been his birthright: the development of an effective infantry rocket launcher. By the spring of 1942, he had hit on the basics of the unit that would eventually go into production. Working with his effective assistant, Edward Uhl, Skinner came up with the idea of a simple hollow tube open on both ends, which, using a rocket, would eliminate all recoil. The trigger device would be electrical, using two D cell flashlight batteries, readily available.

What the two men did not have, however, was a warhead. If the device was to be handled by infantrymen in the field, it had to be kept small, and any amount of high explosive it could deliver to a target would be far too negligible to penetrate armor.

The device they would eventually adopt, far less understandable on an instinctual basis than the rocket motor, was first presented to the U.S. Army's Ordnance Department by a Swiss engineer named Henry Mohaupt. Although Mohaupt claimed to be introducing something new to the ordnance business, what he was suggesting involved a concept discovered some time before, known as the Monroe effect, the focused or hollow charge.

To understand how this works, picture a block of explosive that looks like a brick. If this is put against a large piece of armor two inches thick and exploded, it will probably not be able to break or in any way puncture the armor, which can withstand this kind of general blast.

There is another way, however. In this case, imagine that someone has gouged out a shallow depression in the lengthwise side of the explosive brick, and that this side is placed against the armor plate. After the explosion, the armor would now display in that exact spot an identical depression at an identical depth; in essence, the hollow in the explosive had channeled its force instead of distributing it widely, enabling it to make an impression on the armor plate whereas none had appeared before.

This seems obvious, like child's play, but the implications were enormous, even if no one had ever grasped them before. Take that brick of explosives again, but this time work from the narrow side at the end. Hollow out a deep, deep cone, almost the entire length of the brick. If this side is then put against the armor, and the effect works as it did in the past experiment, theoretically an extremely deep penetration would be made, more than enough to breach two inches of armor. Thus, the magic of the hollow charge.

This in turn led to the unique look of most hollow charge warheads, then and now, which usually looks like two cones—one more pointed than the other—linked wide-base to wide-base and then placed on a long rod. Think about the typical bazooka round, or the modern Soviet-designed RPG (this actually stands for Rocket Antitank Grenade, but most people thinks it's Rocket Propelled Grenade), if you want to get a sense of what this looks like. In this kind of weapon, a large, thin cone of copper is surrounded by explosive. It is attached at its wide base to another cone, which has a much sharper point for aerodynamic purposes and to provide the proper standoff distance. After detonation, the copper will melt and be thrust forward, reversing its shape. What you now have is a thin stream of hot, liquified metal (the scientists actually call it a "warm solid"), traveling at a formidable 30,000 feet per second or so, able to penetrate a considerable amount of armor plate. You can actually make a hollow charge warhead without the liner, but you wind up with a thinner, shallower hole, more like a crater.

And what makes this device so wonderful, so well-suited for an infantry weapon is that velocity is not an issue. In the past, the only conceivable way to breach armor was to use some form of what is now called a penetrator round: get a very hard, pointed projectile to move very fast as the result of a large propelling charge. Its sheer speed and strength—the kinetic energy, in other words—was what did the job. This, however, creates fearsome recoil, requiring elaborate, heavy mountings for the weapon.

But a hollow charge does not depend on kinetic energy, it uses a chemical reaction. Technically, one could throw the darned thing against a tank and as long as the firing pin took and the warhead was at the right angle (good reasons to use a gun instead, not to mention qualms about suicide), the hollow charge reaction would follow and the weapon would work appropriately.

BAZOOKA

By the time Mohaupt showed up with his "secret" invention, the Ordnance Department had already been looking into the development of a hollow charge rifle grenade for the infantry. Skinner found some of these, and from them he finally developed an effective warhead for his rocket launcher.

After successful tests, the Army became excited, and on May 19, 1942 placed an order with the General Electric Company to "design, develop and produce" 5,000 weapons in 30 days, while the E. G. Budd Company was asked to make 25,000 antitank and 5,000 practice rounds. As time became tight, the companies had to rush steel in from Pittsburgh, and even flew some parts in, an unknown luxury at that time. The deadline was met.

It had to be, because it was determined by the need to equip U.S. troops with the weapon before they left for North Africa. By now, as well, it had acquired a name that would stick with it forever, one of the most outlandish of the war. An American jokester, whose name has mercifully been lost to the mists of time, somehow noticed that the new weapon looked quite a bit like an outlandish musical instrument with an absurd moniker, used by the radio comedian Bob Burns. One might think—or at least hope—that with a war going on this anonymous fellow had more important things on his mind, but his eponymous act gave the anti-tank rocket launcher its name: the bazooka. In all fairness, the dubious musical instrument really does bear a remarkable resemblance to the rocket tube named after it.

American troops took to this weapon like they had been born to use it. During the North African landings, one unit was having trouble with a coastal fort, but their bazooka gunner grimly waded ashore, set himself up, and with one shot from his new wonder weapon got the shocked defenders to surrender on the spot. All through that campaign and on into Sicily and Italy, soldiers would now go out and literally stalk their previously dreaded, undefeat-

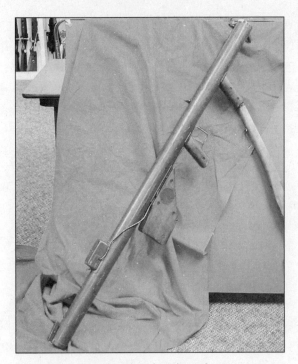

Bazooka (photo by Ed Heasley,
U.S. Army Ordnance Museum, Aberdeen Proving Ground)

able panzer enemy, to the point that one officer said it looked like they were going big-game hunting. Tank after tank fell beneath its prowess, so much so that the Germans came to refer to it as the "shoulder 75." For the first time, infantry had a portable handy weapon that could deal with tanks, instead of the old system of equipping them only with small anti-tank cannon, which were outmoded by then anyway.

The bazooka had its limits, however, and they were becoming all too obvious by 1944 and the invasion of France. Though the weapon was light—it weighed only 13.2 pounds with a 3.4-pound rocket—it could penetrate, at its best, only three inches or so of armor, and by the time Americans faced off against Tigers, Panthers, and even uparmored Mk IVs, it was simply not enough. Now stories, horrible ones, came back of rockets that had no effect on a tank's frontal armor, leaving units helpless and demoralized. One soldier described watching a buddy square off against a Tiger, "It was like he shot the tank with a bloody sparrow. . . . Those big, bloody German tanks; it didn't even take the paint off." One Panther took eleven bazooka hits before it was knocked out by a tank destroyer. This problem would not be fixed until the end of the war, when the Ordnance Department decided to improve on the 2.36 inch bazooka by creating its successor, the much more effective 3.5 inch "super" bazooka. But few, if any, of these arrived in time to help the troops fighting in Europe.[50]

ANTI-TANK RIFLES

Not that the Americans had it all bad; other countries had even worse solutions to the problem of creating an effective infantry anti-tank weapon. The Russians, for example, had developed a successful rocket launcher as early as 1931, but got hung up on the warhead, never turning to the hollow charge, and confronted with the relative feebleness of a regular explosive in so small a package, abandoned the idea.

Instead, they stuck with an earlier concept, a rifle that fired a bullet large enough to penetrate tanks, a notion that barely made sense by the early 1930s, and went downhill from there. These guns fired a 14.5 mm round that, while it had almost double the muzzle energy of a .50 caliber Browning, a formidable figure, to say the least when it came to infantry targets, still paled when faced with armor plate. Penetration was only in the 20 to 25 mm range at normal distances, which by late in the war did not even permit damage to side armor.

Even worse was the size and weight of the gun itself. Wartime pictures really do not show what immense, bulky items these were, but an examination of those on display at the Aberdeen Proving Grounds Museum indicates that they were not the most portable

Russian PTRD anti-tank rifle (photo by Ed Heasley,
U.S. Army Ordnance Museum, Aberdeen Proving Ground)

of items. The first of the Russian anti-tank rifles, the PTRD, was a bolt action weapon that weighed thirty-eight pounds—a handful, even for a two-man crew—and that stretched out to a length of six feet, seven inches. Its successor, the PTRS, was semi-automatic with a five round magazine, but this little device now weighed forty-six pounds and had expanded until it was seven feet long. This was two feet longer than the unwieldy bazooka, not exactly the kind of device most people would want to run around a battlefield with. About the kindest thing that can be said about these things comes from a British weapons expert, "The main conclusion in studying the AT rifles is that they were a considerable waste of time and resources."[51]

PIAT

The British, on the other hand, fielded a weapon that while a lot more effective, was equally outlandish in some ways. Their Projector, Infantry, Anti-Tank—always referred to as a PIAT—carried a

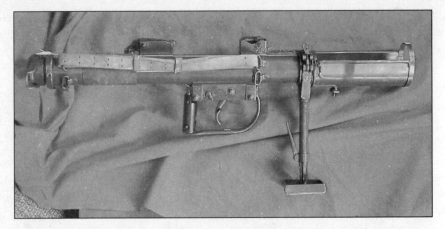

PIAT (photo by Ed Heasley, U.S. Army Ordnance Museum, Aberdeen Proving Ground)

comparable warhead to that of the bazooka, but was an infinitely more difficult weapon to use in combat. First of all, it weighed thirty-two pounds (compared to thirteen pounds for the bazooka), a fact that by itself was enough to discourage anyone from wanting to lug it about.

Far, far worse was the firing mechanism, which depended on an extremely heavy spring. In order to cock this mechanical device, a soldier, faced with an oncoming armored vehicle, had to stand up and place his feet on a huge crossbar at the end of the PIAT, then pull the rest of this heavy weapon upward, against enormous resistance, until finally it locked the firing mechanism into place. This required an unbelievable 200 pounds of pressure, the equivalent of bench pressing one-tenth of a ton; even more wearisome, there were instructions on how to do it from a prone position!

After that the real fun began. Upon firing the trigger, that horrendous spring was released, setting off the charges in the tail boom, which would fire with sufficient force to actually recock the mechanism, which must have been a most distasteful feeling to experience. Ian Hogg told the memorable story of Fusillier Jefferson in Italy, who dashed out into the open and fired his PIAT twice from the hip, knocking out two Tiger tanks and winning himself the Victoria Cross. As Hogg so delightfully—and insightfully—puts it, "the general opinion in the ranks was that he deserved it for firing the thing from the hip, let alone killing two tanks with it."[52]

GERMANY: FAILURE AND SUCCESS

The Germans arguably, came up with the worst anti-tank weapon of them all, not because it was ungainly, but because it was so futile. This was the Sturmpistole, a flare gun made overly elaborate with bubble sights and a folding stock. It fired a hollow charge grenade with a tiny—as in miniature—warhead that weighed one-quarter of an ounce. A great weapon for knocking down, say an armored doll house, but nothing a sane soldier would use to tackle a tank.

The Germans made up for it, and then some, with another device. After seeing the bazooka in action, they created their own version, the panzerschreck. This was inadequate, however, since on the Russian front they were facing blitzkrieg as they had never imagined it, with superior Russian tanks attacking at all times, and from all points of the compass. It would not be enough to merely have trained anti-tank teams using a sophisticated weapon; every soldier had to be capable of fighting these vehicles.

To this aim, Dr. Langweiler of Hugo Schneider Ag of Leipzig came up with a fairly radical concept. Langweiler developed a weapon that began with a sheet metal steel tube 31.5 inches long, with the most primitive firing device imaginable at the top, just a hinged metal bar that pushed down into the tube to activate the circuit. The projectile had a hollow charge warhead mounted on a wooden rod, to which were attached four steel fins that would deploy on release, providing stability in flight; the propellant charge was inside the tube itself. After firing, a soldier just discarded the empty tube and picked up a new, fully loaded one and went on. It was so simple any infantryman, any person, could use it, with almost no training at all; just point and shoot, possibly destroying a tank. The Germans called it the panzerfaust.

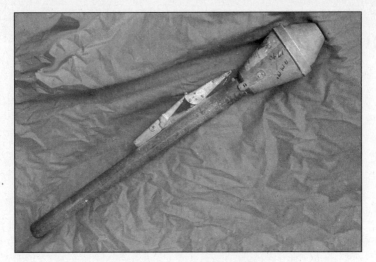

Panzerfaust (photo by Ed Heasley,
U.S. Army Ordnance Museum, Aberdeen Proving Ground)

This was, to put it mildly, a crude and ugly weapon, and one that took almost as much courage to use, at first, as the PIAT. Original range was only thirty meters, which meant a soldier had to get awfully close to a tank to hit it, during which time its crew might take notice of his presence and attempt to discourage the lad. Armor penetration, however, was far better than anything the Allies had, 140 mm on armor angled at 30 degrees.

After that the Germans started to refine the weapon, and it just got better. Range increased to 150 meters and penetration was now up to 200 mm, or eight inches, more armor than most seafaring cruisers mounted at that point in the war. Put another way, no Allied tank, even the heavy Russian ones, could stand before it. Studies showed it could penetrate the front armor of the Panther tank, something a bazooka gunner could not dream of doing.

A WINNER

Which was the best infantry anti-tank weapon of World War II? The bazooka gets special notice because it was the pioneer, the first of its kind, the one that introduced one of the most important concepts in ground warfare. There is no question, for example, that it is the most *important* weapon in its class. Following the notion of generations, it was also the best in the early part of the war.

By 1944, however, its day had passed. Whereas the bazooka required a trained, two-man crew to use, the panzerfaust could be used effectively by every common soldier, and was so simple to operate that no special instruction was required; you just pointed the warhead, holding the tube on the shoulder, or even tucking it under one's arm. It was also literally foolproof, and if one of the launchers failed, you just picked up another; they were so cheap to make, everyone could be issued with several of them. While later critics decried its crudity, this superior concept would be borrowed by the West years later to create the Light Anti-Weapon Rocket, or LAW. The Russians copied a later version of the panzerfaust that could actually be reloaded, to produce the RPG-1, which eventually led to the now ubiquitous RPG-7. Thus, some of the most well-known tank busters of today—on both sides of the former Iron Curtain—are descendants of the panzerfaust.

How effective was this? The men of Company K, U.S. Army, in the famous book by that name, reported that the panzerfaust was "a more efficient and powerful weapon than our bazooka," a statement tanker Belton Cooper agreed with as well. One test conducted by Captain John Roller of the U.S. Army involved firing a bazooka and a panzerfaust at a burned out Sherman tank at 100 yards. The bazooka made a hole about 1.5 inches in size, while the panzerfaust ripped open a gap 2.75 inches in diameter.[53]

Most telling of all are the figures for Russian tank losses of their T-34 tanks. Throughout the war, the majority of these came from German anti-tank guns, with panzerfausts not being a factor until late 1944, and even then these weapons usually accounted for less than 10 percent of the Russian losses.

But then came Berlin, a battle of horrific ferocity, fought at close quarters by a Wehrmacht down to its last surviving, often poorly trained and desperate soldiers. In this kind of environment, the panzerfaust came truly into its own, and Russian sources claim that almost 23 percent of their T-34 losses came from this one weapon. The Germans made over 8 million panzerfausts, and it was Allied tankers, like the Russians fighting in Berlin, who paid the heavy price these innovative weapons exacted from their foes.

PART II

TANKS

7

Defining Greatness

WHAT MAKES A TANK the best? Whenever I ask a class, the first hands that shoot up come from students who all have the same answer, something like "a big gun." Firepower, in other words, for those a bit more articulate. And they're wrong.

Once I have made that point clear, the next volley all deals with armor, the thicker the better. Still wrong.

There is usually silence now, and soon someone else mentions speed. Still wrong, but like the others, an important part of the answer.

What makes a tank the best, instead, is *balance*. All armored vehicles make use of three criteria: firepower, armor, and speed. A tank has to kill the enemy, it has to be protected, and it has to move. All of these are relevant.

The problem is that these factors are often at odds with one another; too much emphasis on any one aspect renders a tank practically worthless. An increase in armor or firepower, for example, can only come by making the tank heavier and/or bigger, thus causing a reduction in mobility. Too much of that, and you wind up with a machine that really cannot partake in armored warfare, and that will soon be cut off and destroyed. If, for example, during an attack medium tanks and armored personnel carriers are moving 20 miles per hour (mph), and the heavy tanks only 7 mph, they will soon be left behind. At that stage, they are no longer supporting the attack and are left without infantry protection, open to all manner of assault. Of course, you can increase engine size, but that necessitates a bigger tank, with more armor, and the law of diminishing returns starts to set in. And on we go.

All sorts of problems can—and did—occur when designers ignored balance. What happens when you increase the size of the gun, but decrease the armor plate in proportion, to keep up speed? The answer is simple: you get a tank that can knock out a lot of other tanks, but is terribly, terribly vulnerable, and may well be destroyed before it gets a chance to use its superior weapon.

Then there is the reverse scenario: a tank with thick armor plate and too small a gun. If anyone thinks this is all hypothetical, that is exactly what happened with the British Matilda, which for a while had the thickest armor on the North African battlefield. Unfortunately, designers had installed a very small turret ring, meaning it could only take a 2 Pounder gun (about 40 mm), which at that point was barely effective. German shells might have popped off the Matilda's thick frontal plates, but unless it got awfully close, all the poor gunners could do was run around firing minor projectiles that did little or no damage to their enemies either. Quite a frustrating image, to say the least.

The best tank, therefore, is one that balances these three attributes perfectly, that provides some kind of platonic symmetry that adds up to a superlative fighting machine that does everything well, and that provides, in the end, a totality that far exceeds the sum of its parts.

Before we start to explore and evaluate who fielded what and how they stacked up in this analysis, we need to make some adjustments to our criteria before we move on. In recent years, analysts have substituted new terms, more meaningful ones, for the trinity of firepower, armor, and speed, and one of them applies here as well.

Instead of firepower, the term now in use is lethality, and it makes a lot of sense. In a modern, main battle tank (MBT), the ability to score on a target is only in part a product of its ordnance. Sensors of every kind now make all the difference, especially in less than ideal conditions, such as darkness or smoke. Lethality, therefore, refers to a tank's *total* capability for destroying the enemy, and is much more appropriate to modern warfare.

The simple term "armor" has also been replaced by a more comprehensive term: survivability. For years now, tanks have been protected by more than steel plates, with new ideas coming out seemingly every day. Armor, itself, for example, is rarely just simple metal anymore, let alone steel. Most Western tanks use a highly classified Chobham armor that involves extensive use of ceramics, and is strengthened by a depleted uranium mesh. Versions of the former Soviet Bloc's T-72, on the other hand, placed layers of sand, quartz, and especially glass-reinforced fibers between sheets of conventional steel.

Beyond that, there are a host of other new ideas that have redefined how a tank protects itself. Reactive armor, for example, involves covering a tank with small, easily replaced plates containing a sandwich of metal "bread" with an explosive charge filling. These are designed to disrupt projectiles, and are especially effective against the hot stream of a hollow charge warhead. The Russians have even gone a step further by developing several systems of *active* armor, which detect an incoming projectile and then fire a cloud of steel balls to deflect it. While there are still problems, large American weapons companies are beginning to take a look at this idea, purchasing some of these in the now open weapons markets so they can run tests of their own.

The last new term is availability, which has replaced the traditional "speed." This denotes a number of factors that really should have been used long ago.

In truth, the criteria really being evaluated here is the ability to get an armored vehicle onto the battlefield, and its capacity for maneuver once it gets there. How fast it moves is an obvious component of this, but so is mechanical reliability. If a tank breaks down all the time, it will not be available, will not take part in any effort to win. Even production becomes a factor here: a tank that takes ten times as much time and precious materials to produce (1,000 percent) but works only 50 percent better is a loser. The ability to make a tank available in large numbers on the battlefield, therefore, a matter of design and manufacture, also becomes part of the equation for this criterion.

Thus, while lethality and survivability both speak to post-World War II technology, availability is an appropriate issue to evaluate here, as it seriously affected the excellence of tanks in that struggle and helped determine the outcome of battles, if not the war itself. Accordingly, we will take it into account in our discussions as well.

8

GERMAN TANKS: THE FIRST GENERATIONS

ANY STUDY OF TANKS in World War II has to start with the German machines, because they introduced to the world the modern form of tank warfare. Blitzkrieg stunned the West, proving itself capable of the most startling feats of arms imaginable. Generals descended from those who had led armies for four long years on the battlefields of France and Belgium now found themselves defeated in a matter of months, something that seemed beyond comprehension.

To most observers back then, the weapon, more than any other, that had seemed to produce that victory was the tank. More than the screaming Stuka, more than the flashing 88, it was the massed wedge of armor that captured the imagination: a vista of tanks everywhere, cascading across the landscape, rolling over, grinding over every and any obstacle the Allies could produce. Tanks, more tanks, endless tanks became the image that dominated the thinking of the West, as its military leaders devised concepts on how to defeat the German enemy.

And that, of course, was strange, because in truth the machines were not really that amazing, although their tactics most definitely were. Tank expert Bryan Perrett went even further, claiming that, "because of the spectacular . . . victories from 1939 to 1941, it is tempting to regard Hitler's Panzerwaffe as a superbly equipped cutting edge for the rest of the army. In reality, the Panzerwaffe excelled only in technique, and was very badly equipped."[1]

PANZER MK I

The story of German World War II tanks begins, of course, with the rearmament program that actually originated in 1932, even before the Nazis took power. That year the army laid out specifications for an armored vehicle and asked five German firms to submit prototypes, hiding the project under the rubric that they were asking for models of "agricultural tractors."

Wehrmacht officials were under no illusions as to what they were ordering. At this early stage, they could not expect to get anything that could even vaguely go up against a Western armored force. Instead, they sought a training tank, something basic and simple that could be used to teach troops of the emergent Panzer divisions how to handle such vehicles, as well as helping to develop new tactics. When war came, they could be used in the reconnaissance role as well. This was the PzKpfw Mk I, or Panzer Mk I.

Before we go any further, it is probably useful to clarify some misunderstood terms. The term "panzer" is literally nothing more than the German word for "armor," and that is all it means. A German panzer, for example, simply means a German tank, and a panzer division is the equivalent of an American armored division. This is altogether different, however, from the Panther, a specific model of German tank whose formal designation was PzKpfw Mark V. The term "PzKpfw," by the way, is simply an abbreviation for "panzerkampfwagen," or armored fighting vehicle.

The Panzer Mk I was basic and simple indeed, barely a tankette. Weighing about six tons, it had only a two-man crew, and its armor plate ranged from 6 to 13 mm—only half an inch at its thickest point—barely enough to stop small arms fire. Armament in its entirety consisted of two rifle-caliber machine guns. At its tallest point, furthermore, the tank was less than five feet, eight inches high. Stop and think of how tall you are, and then consider what it meant to stand next to, let alone be inside this size cabin. Most people consider tanks to be huge, powerful vehicles, but some perspective is gained by the fact that in the American clothing industry, men who are less than five feet, eight inches usually require short sizes in suits; it is kind of shocking, in other words, to stand next to a tank that you are taller than. The Mk I looks like a dwarf, for example, when placed next to a standard World War I tank, even though it was supposed to be much more advanced.

German officials recognized this tank for what it was (although it would be used extensively in the early years of the war, and not just for reconnaissance); and while they had already laid plans for the primary vehicles of the proposed panzer armies, what would become the Mks III and IV, they recognized that they needed something a bit stronger in the interim, and that was the PzKpfw Mk II.

Panzer Mk I (Thomas M. Tencza)

PANZER MK II

This was a much better proposition, but hardly a match for tanks being built in France, Russia, or Britain. Weight increased to almost ten tons, with frontal armor of 15 mm, which would later be increased to 35 mm by the addition of supplementary plates. More important, it was the first German tank to pack something more than a machine gun, being armed with one 20 mm cannon and one 7.9 mm machine gun. The former fed from ten-round magazines, eighteen of which were carried, and had a rate of fire of 280 rpm. While in no way could this tear open the front armor of any Allied medium tank, even of the 1930s generation, it could inflict damage on sides and rear, and it was deadly to the infantry carriers and tankettes common in that era. The armor, while superior to the Mk I—which was not saying much—was still vulnerable to even the most basic antitank cannon of that era, weapons in the 37 to 40 mm class.

Panzer Mk II (Thomas M. Tencza)

But both of these were stopgaps. The Wehrmacht expected them to fill out the ranks and allow for training and maneuvers, but the tanks they planned to fight a war with were the Mks III and IV.

For the German army, each of these tanks performed a specific battlefield function that would complement the other, creating the perfect fighting combination that should prove unbeatable. The breakdown was simple: the Mk III would be the anti-tank weapon, the panzer used to fight other tanks, and would be equipped with a smaller caliber, long-barreled, high-velocity cannon with good armor penetration. The Mk IV, on the other hand, was the infantry's tank, and would carry a larger caliber, short-barrel weapon with a powerful high explosive round that was more suited to destroying fortifications.

DEFINING TERMS: BARREL LENGTH

Before we go any further, we need to talk about tank terms; in particular, the nomenclature used to describe their primary armament, the main cannon.

In general, heavy guns are measured two ways: by the diameter of the hole in the barrel, and by the barrel's length as well. The first tells us something about the relative size and weight of a round, the second tells us about the velocity and accuracy of a projectile, since a longer barrel shoots faster and straighter. Diameter is the more familiar concept, and can be grasped all the way down to small arms, from the .30 caliber machine gun to the 88 mm cannon on a Tiger tank.

But length is a more complex calculation, and has to be discussed in context. A three foot long barrel means one thing on a .30 caliber machine gun, but something far different for a 75 mm tank gun. In the first it is standard, but on the second it would be ludicrously short. Thus, it is more important to know not only how long a barrel is in absolute terms, but how long it is *relative to the size of the munition.*

As a result, the standard term to describe a gun's length is that of "caliber," a rather confusing notion, since this is also employed, in a totally different way, to describe the diameter of small arms.[2] When used on tank guns, instead, it means the length of a barrel measured in *how many times bigger it is than the diameter of the shell*. A 75 mm tank gun, for example, fires a projectile that is three inches across. If the barrel was twelve feet long, it would be forty-eight times that measurement, and as a result would be referred to as an L/48, or more accurately as a 75 mm L/48 cannon.

As a general rule, the longer the barrel, the better, as this provides greater speed to the round (the gas is acting on it for a longer time), and more accuracy. Barrels in the L/25 to L/40 range are considered short, less powerful, and less accurate weapons and are used to fire high explosive rounds instead of anti-tank rounds; these are primarily used in tanks designed to knock out fortifications, to act on behalf of the infantry mopping up these obstacles. Cannon in the L/40 to L/60 range are considered of medium strength, and anything above that, such as the 75 mm L/70 gun on the Panther, represents an extremely high velocity, extremely powerful weapon, capable of long distance tank killing.

PANZER MK III

Back to the German tanks. By 1936, the order for Mk III prototypes, the tank that would tackle and destroy other tanks, had already gone out. On the all-critical issue of firepower, the panzer commanders wanted a 50 mm gun, but ordnance pointed out that 37 mm was the standard anti-tank weapon used by the infantry, so a compromise was reached: they would install a 37 mm L/45 gun on the Mk III, but allow a slightly larger turret ring, one big enough to accept the 50 mm gun later on.

As finally produced, the Mk III was really a good, basic fighting tank, with conventional interior arrangements consisting of the driving compartment in the front, the fighting compartment in the

Panzer Mk III (photo by author, U.S. Army Ordnance Museum, Aberdeen Proving Ground)

middle, and the engine in the rear; accommodations were reasonably generous for the five-man crew. Prototypes used an engine that provided a top speed of approximately 20 mph; later versions used a better engine that took this up to 25 mph, but that must have gone down later as extra armor got added on, increasing the weight by several tons.

That armor started at 15 mm on the prototypes, but the first Mk IIIs to go into battle in 1939 all had 30 mm frontal armor. This was not enough, however, and the panzer commanders soon knew it. The Model H, therefore, fielded in 1940, incorporated another 30 mm in bolted-on armor, with a revised suspension to take the extra weight. This modification was later incorporated into the Model J, which had a solid 50 mm armor on the front, and even this would eventually be augmented by armor plates, in an effort to keep the Mk III viable after the Germans encountered the powerful Russian tanks.

The Model G was also the first upgunned version, incorporating a 50 mm L/42 cannon, which was really not that good a thing to do at all, for a number of reasons. Adolf Hitler had ruled—quite wisely, in this case—that the Mk III should have a long barreled gun capable of knocking out enemy tanks easily. The L/42 gun had relatively modest velocity, was not capable of the job it had been set to accomplish, and it also made Hitler very, very mad—never a smart or good thing to do.

Finally, with the Model J, the Mk III got a 50 mm L/60 weapon capable of doing some good; whereas the L/42 round traveled at only 2,250 feet per second and could only penetrate 49 mm of armor set at 30 degrees at a range of 500 yards, the L/60 could do substantially better: a muzzle velocity of 2,700 feet per second enabled it to penetrate 60 mm of armor under the same conditions. Compared to the weapons of other countries' tanks, especially the Russian vehicles—as the Germans would soon find out—this was still barely adequate, but a lot better than anything else the Germans had at the time.

This made the Mk III their prime tank, a fact lost to the mists of time. The Mk III now has a poor, or at last limited reputation; after the invasion of Russia, it quickly became obsolete. But during the halcyon years of the panzer divisions, 1939–1941, and the campaigns in Poland, France, and Russia, the generals considered the Mk III the most important tank they had, the hard hitting weapon that stood at the very tip of the spear. It was widely regarded as a better vehicle, in automotive terms, than the far more famous Mk IV, and while the various armaments would prove inadequate in Russia, even the low velocity 50 mm L/42 outranged the standard British tank gun, the two pounder. The Mk III was also fully equipped with radios in each tank, something that took the Russians a long time to achieve, which gave it a great deal of tactical superiority. From 1939 to 1941, it was the vehicle the Germans used to implement fast-moving blitzkrieg tactics that could knock out any enemy. As Bryan Perrett noted, "During the high years of blitzkrieg it was the only weapon in the German arsenal that really counted ... the fact remains that it was the PzKpfw III that brought Hitler closest to achieving his wildest dreams."[3]

PANZER MK IV

The real star of the early panzer series, however, was the Mk IV, although no one knew it at the time. In the original vision, the Mk IV was supposed to be secondary to the Mk III, in that it was never perceived as a breakthrough tank. Instead, it would deal with those obstacles that the fast moving panzer forces either could not avoid or else had left behind; to do this it was equipped with a short-barreled 75 mm L/24 gun, one that could fire a much larger high explosive shell than anything a Mk III could ever deliver, albeit not very far nor very fast. This was, in other words, reasonably effective for knocking out fortifications, but not nearly so potent when it came to defeating enemy armor. The standard German tank battalion at the beginning of the war was supposed to consist of four companies; three would be made up of Mk IIIs, and only the last would have Mk IVs, to be used in support.

But the designers of the Mk IV did one thing that made it special: they provided a very large turret ring, relative to its size.

People who have never been inside a tank tend to forget that the larger their armament becomes, the more it extends *inside* the turret, as well as outside. It is sort of like building a model kit, in which the tank gun is a thin piece of plastic, but nothing ever protrudes into a turret that no one ever sees inside of anyway.

In real life, however, a larger gun takes up *a lot* of space in the turret, and especially extends a lot further back, if for no other reason than because of the necessity to keep it in balance. A rifle-caliber machine gun, for example, operated by a single gunner, requires a turret about thirty inches in diameter. Move up to a 37 mm gun with a coaxial machine gun and a two man crew, and the design now requires a forty-five inch turret ring. A 75 mm gun moves this up to sixty inches, and the 88 mm or 90 mm cannon found by mid to late war necessitated tanks with seventy inch turret rings, almost six feet. Thus, what appears to the non-specialist as an arcane matter—how big to design the turret opening in the hull—becomes a critical factor in a tank's effective lifetime in the fast changing technological environment of all-out war. And though this now seems rather obvious—the U.S. Army's M1 Abrams started with a 105 mm gun, but was designed to take a 120 mm, and will probably move to a larger weapon than that without trouble—in the years preceding World War II this was not really thought about all that much. The British Matilda, as mentioned, had superior armor, but could only mount a tiny gun because of this failure of vision.

Because of this unique qualification, the Mk IV became one of the great stalwarts of the war; not the Germans' greatest tank, not their flashiest or most famous, but the one that held up the best of them all. In the long run, the Mk IV was the only tank Germany

Panzer Mk IV with 75 mm L/24 gun (photo by author,
U.S. Army Ordnance Museum, Aberdeen Proving Ground)

Panzer Mk IV with 75 mm L/48 gun (photo by author,
U.S. Army Ordnance Museum, Aberdeen Proving Ground)

produced throughout the entire war, some of them fighting in
Poland in September 1939, while the last models came off the
assembly line practically as Berlin fell. Because of this, more of
them also appeared on the battlefield than any other German
machine, making it numerically the most common tank encountered by the Allies.

Thus, more than any other tank of the war, the Mk IV became
a story of adaptation and development. The early versions, Ausfs
A to D, were equipped with the short barreled 75 mm gun and had
frontal armor of up to 30 mm (the Ausfs A actually began with
only 20 mm on the turret and 15 mm on the hull front).

By 1939, however, the German Panzer Corps was being tested
in the reality of full scale war, and the thin armor plate of even the
Mk IIIs and IVs—let alone the Is and IIs—was found wanting. By
December 1939 add-on armor was being fitted to what became the
Ausf E, but this was only a stopgap, and in the spring of 1941, just
in time for Russia, the Ausf F began to appear. This incorporated
from the start 50 mm armor on the hull and turret front. Even more
important, later models began to be built with a very different gun

altogether, a 75 mm L/43, which gave the Mk IV a vastly increased anti-armor ability.

But by then the Germans were mired in Russia, facing vastly superior tanks. In an effort to keep the Mk IV viable, designers went back to add on armor in the Ausf G, and by the later runs were putting in the best gun this tank would ever feature, a 75 mm L/48 that could fire an armor-piercing round with a muzzle velocity of 2,461 feet per second. Later models started to lose their all-around capability as the Germans became desperate; the Ausf H and Ausf J had 80 mm of frontal armor that added so much weight on a modest platform and engine that the speed dropped as low as 10 mph on anything but level, hardpacked roads. Not exactly a weapon of lightning warfare, anymore, the Mk IV still fought on, later with added skirts and a turret bustle to defend against hollow charge weapons. The Ausf H actually became the most numerous variant of them all.

In the end, more than 10,500 Mk IV chassis were built; 7,000 were used to make tanks, the rest going into specialized vehicles like a variety of different self-propelled guns. It fought on every front, in very battle, and, according to virtually every commentator, it became the most important German tank of the war, the true backbone of the panzer corps.

But despite this record and longevity, the Mk IV always was, and always would remain, a conventional design out of the 1930s, with slabsided, vertical armor, and the traditional layout inside. One of its more progressive features was an electric motor for traversing the turret, but even this had to be abandoned as the weight got higher because of added armor, and was given up in the Ausf J. Beyond that, its greatest strength was its adaptability and general ruggedness, as opposed to any kind of innovation.

Put another way, the Mk IV was nowhere near the best tank of the war, and was in many ways a retrograde design, even by 1939. How then did the Germans manage the great blitzkrieg victories of 1939–1941?

TACTICS

Before we answer this question—with all that it tells about the relative merits of German tanks of this period—we must first explore
even further, to demonstrate just what kind of an answer is
required. Between September 1939 and December 1941, the Germans achieved what are still believed to be three of the greatest
feats of armored warfare ever accomplished: the victory over
Poland in a matter of weeks in September 1939; the taking of
France in the summer of 1940; and the first months in Russia,
from July to December 1941, when the Wehrmacht made it from
the border almost to Moscow, a distance of hundreds of miles over
an extended front, in a matter of mere months, against the largest
army in the world at the time.

What makes this record even more astounding is the breakdown of the tanks they used to accomplish these gains. The
German General Staff planned to fight World War II with a fleet
made up almost exclusively of Mk III and IV tanks, with the Mk II
used for reconnaissance, and the Mk I either fazed out completely
or else retained for training purposes only; because of this plan,
they expected to wait until 1942 or 1943 before initiating hostilities. Hitler wanted war sooner than that, however, so the generals
caved in, despite their misgivings, and overlooked massive struc-
tural problems, especially in the area of logistical support.

Thus, what makes the early victories so amazing, from a
modern-day standpoint, was the mix of armor the Germans used to
carry out these feats. In Poland, the Germans attacked with 1,445
Mk Is, 1,223 Mk IIs, 98 Mk IIIs, and 211 Mk IVs. Put another way,
almost half of the attacking force consisted of training tanks with
nothing more than a pair of 7.9 mm machine guns. What should
have been the mainstay of the force, the Mk IIIs and Mk IVs, combined made up only 10 percent of the total, and the Mk III, which
was supposed to bear the brunt of the fighting, was a paltry 3 percent of the invasion force.

By Spring 1940 in France, the Germans had gotten better, but so had their enemy. The panzer count was now: Mk I, 523; Mk II, 955; Mk III, 349; Mk IV, 278; captured Czech tanks (comparable to the Mk III), 334—for a total of 2,439. Once again, the inferior models—Mk Is and IIs—made up the bulk of the force, 1,478 against 961 of the other, more sophisticated tanks. Furthermore, of the Mk IIIs, none had yet been upgunned, so they still carried the 37 mm cannon, the least effective weapon this tank was ever equipped with.

And what makes the German victory even more astounding—this is referring, by the way, to the conquest of France and the defeat of the French *and* British armies in a matter of months—is the fact that the Western Allies not only had more tanks, but *better* ones. The French put over 3,330 tanks in the field, and the British contributed another 310, 100 of them being heavy infantry tanks. German tanks were just introducing 30 mm armor and still used 37 mm guns but the French Char B1 and Somua S-35 had 50 to 60 mm of frontal armor, and a 47 mm anti-tank cannon that was the most powerful of its class on the Western front, second in the world only to what the Russians were fielding in their models at this time.

This amazing pattern held true to form in Russia. In July 1941, the Germans attacked with 410 Mk Is, 746 Mk IIs, 965 Mk IIIs, 439 Mk IVs, and 772 Czech tanks, admittedly a vast improvement on anything they had ever fielded before—finally, the Mk Is and IIs were in a minority—but they faced a Russian tank park of over *20,000* tanks, some of which were very good, indeed. Nevertheless, for several months, the Wehrmacht proved unstoppable, and made it across hundreds of miles of steppe almost to the capital in Moscow.[4]

Keep in mind that these will always remain the greatest victories of the Wehrmacht; nothing it ever did *after* the introduction of the famous tanks—the Tigers and Panthers—comes anywhere near to these achievements, and in fact, by that time the Germans were fighting defensively, losing ground, not taking it.

Thus, a very basic, critically important point is being made here. Put as baldly as possible: the Wehrmacht did not win—when it was really winning—because it had good tanks. Its best were not as good as the Allies', and the Germans at this time were often using mostly inferior models anyway. As Perrett succinctly put it, "the Germans were out-numbered, out-gunned and under-armored," which seems to cover all aspects of their technical infe-riority, neatly enough.[5]

So how did they achieve what seemed frankly impossible just prior to the outbreak of hostilities? The answer lies in tactics, how the machines were used, not the qualities of the machines them-selves, which were secondary at best.

When World War II broke out, countries like Britain and France shared certain assumptions as to how armor should be employed. They believed that a first-rate army maintained two kinds of tanks: infantry and cavalry. The first would be employed for the break-through, and their design and deployment was appropriate: in gen-eral, these were large, slow, machines, and they would be dispersed up and down the front, one at a time, with no concentration of force. Moving at the same pace as the infantry (some of these tanks went less than ten miles an hour), they were heavily armored, and could withstand the fiery march across no man's land till it came time to grapple directly with the enemy's line. Here, their fire-power would overcome the resistance, working with the infantry, creating a hole in the enemy line. At this point the cavalry tanks—fast, lightly armored and armed—would move out to quickly exploit these gains, much as their mounted predecessors had done in prior centuries.

If this idea seems old fashioned or doomed to failure, think about how reasonable it seems. Most images we have of tanks, for example, out of the movies from the World War II–era and beyond, show exactly this kind of formation: the line of men moving ahead with some tanks in support.

A few British thinkers came up with an alternative model, but not many of the generals listened. One of the exceptions, however, was Heinz Guderian, head of the panzer troops in Germany and the greatest tactical genius of armored force ever put on this earth; Guderian is truly the founder of modern tank warfare.

Guderian argued that instead of spreading out his machines, they should be massed together in an iron hammer that would be virtually invincible; *"Klotzen nicht Kleckern"* he used to say: "Don't feel with the fingers but hit with the fist." No front could handle armor when it was used in this way, as a steel package, rather than as a series of tiny envelopes of limited thrusting power. Mass the tanks, and a breakthrough was inevitable. One British vet of North Africa wrote that he seemed to always be facing "a solid embattled column with the heavy panzers at the head of the battering ram," calling it "a phalanx of destruction."[6]

After that, Guderian believed, everything was mobility. The tanks' greatest asset, he felt, was that it could move fast with armored firepower, and the moment momentum slowed, that attribute would be lost, possibly along with the battle. If obstacles stood in one's way—strong points that could not be easily overcome—leave them behind and let the ponderous infantry divisions following behind deal with them.* Always thrust, always move, until the enemy is cut off, surrounded, and destroyed.

Guderian designed the entire army around this need for mobility, for what would soon be called "blitzkrieg" or "lightning warfare." Infantry had to keep up with the tanks to provide support, so they had to be motorized. The armored personnel carrier was far away in the distant future, and Germany even lacked a strong contingent of half-tracks, so Guderian saw to it that each panzer division in the early days had a battalion of motorcycle troops with sidecars, guaranteeing that a nucleus of foot soldiers would be available no matter how fast the tanks moved. Self-propelled artillery, similarly, was in its earliest stages, so instead the Germans used aerial firepower: the Stuka dive bombers became their field pieces,

---

*Infantry commanders just loved this idea, as one might imagine.

knocking out obstacles just as any howitzer would, but able to keep pace with the fast moving columns. All of this required the best radio communications possible, and officers were also expected to remain close to the front and stay in charge amidst rapidly changing conditions. Even the tanks shifted design to fit this scheme, as the Mk III started gradually to move to what would later be known as a main battle tank, an all-purpose vehicle strong enough to take on other tanks, but fast enough to fight a battle of exploitation and mobility.

No other nation thought like this, set up its forces like this, or designed tanks like this. French tanks, for example, may have had better armor and guns, but they usually had one-man turrets, which meant a slow rate of fire and difficulty in keeping up with a fast moving battlefront. Russian tanks had no radios, so they would find it much harder to fight a war where quick, subtle changes in command were critical at every level. Both French and British tanks were supposed to move at the pace of walking men burdened by heavy equipment, and as late as 1930 the French Army's *Instruction on the Employment of Tanks* began with the clear, seemingly unassailable statement, "The tank is an infantry-supporting weapon." Worst of all, they were sent to the front in penny-packets, easy pickings when a large armored force appeared and rolled over them.[7]

And if the Allies lacked inspiration (at least at the earlier stages of the war; they would learn hard lessons, fast), the Germans were very, very good at these new tactics. The tank brigade of a panzer division would attack on a front of no more than 5,000 yards (less than 3 miles), with the Mk IIIs in the front (especially if enemy tanks were to be encountered), the Mk Is and IIs moving out to the side, and the Mk IVs behind, using their short 75 mms as artillery over the heads of their own front line to knock out recalcitrant pockets. Massed firepower in a single place made the difference, and the brute weight and then the speed of the attack carried it past the enemy line, back toward loftier objectives, such as headquarters elements, or a maneuver of encirclement that could trap and destroy an entire army.[8]

Thus, the *impression* the blitzkrieg gave was of overwhelming armored force, irresistible, sweeping everything before it. French and British soldiers carried images of tanks and more tanks, endless waves of tanks, that left them powerless; in some areas just a cry that the panzers were on the way was enough to make a line break and run. Why not, if nothing could stop this juggernaut? Even later in the war, an American wrote in an Intelligence Bulletin, "I never saw a German tank employed singly." Former British prime minister David Lloyd-George observed that this was, "A very remarkable war! Over on the German side there are no men . . . just machines!"[9]

There were, of course, problems even with these tactics. One was that it depended on lots of tanks; the notion of a mass of armor was critical to this approach. Yet, even during the great victories, the panzer divisions were taking serious casualties, which, while nowhere in proportion to what they were inflicting on their opponents, were still not easily replaced. Another problem was that this system was truly based on momentum, a rolling column that moved so fast and so unexpectedly that it could bowl over superior forces with surprise and local firepower superiority. If it stalled, on the other hand (which is why the panzer officers were always told to go around obstacles), the tide might easily turn against them, with even their best tanks undergunned and underarmed. When this did happen, German panzer units could, and did, suffer terrible defeats.

Above all, there was the biggest danger of them all, that someone else could use the same tactics against the Wehrmacht. That would come, in time, as the Allies East and West learned the lessons of blitzkrieg and then applied them. But before that time, the Germans had to meet and deal with a startling problem, namely being technologically overmatched to a degree they never dreamed possible.

9

RUSSIAN TANKS:
WAR WINNERS

WHEN GERMANY INVADED RUSSIA, the Russian tank force consisted of mostly obsolete models, which got wiped out in record numbers. In the first few months of combat, Russia lost more tanks—about 13,000—than the rest of the world's armies, combined, had tanks.

But at the same time, new designs were coming off the production lines, headed by the amazing T-34. In its several variations, it can clearly be stated that this was the weapon that won the armored struggle in World War II.

BACKGROUND

The Soviet Union had long been interested in armored formations, the first tank regiment being formed, on an experimental basis, in 1927 in Moscow, using sixty foreign tanks. Far more important, however, were the ideas of Mikhail Tukhachevsky, Field Marshall and Chief of the General Staff of the Russian army. Tukhachevsky, on his own, evolved ideas even more advanced than Guderian's, calling for combined arms forces based on armored units to be created in large numbers, which would engage in fast moving "deep operations" to cut off and destroy large enemy units. In late 1932 the Russians formed their first armored corps, three years before the Germans started building panzer divisions. As David Glantz and Jonathan House, two of the foremost historians of the Russian army in World War II, wrote, "in the mid-1930s, the Soviet Union led the world in production, planning, and fielding of mechanized forces . . . the Red Army was well ahead of its German counterparts in both theoretical concepts and practical experience of mechanized warfare."[10]

In 1937, however, Tukhachevsky caught Josef Stalin's eye, as the dictator was in the midst of purging the army in order to make sure they could not threaten his hegemony, and that year the general was arrested and executed. His ideas, however, lived on, in two forms. One was the Russians' skill at operational warfare, a middle level between tactical (practiced by local field officers) and strategic (decided by world leaders), that involved senior commanders moving large bodies of troops in campaigns of encirclement and extermination. This was demonstrated, for example, both at the encirclement of the German Sixth Army at Stalingrad in 1942–1943, and later in 1944 with the destruction of Army Group Center during Operation Bagration, the greatest land victory of World War II.[11]

The other aspect of Tukhachevsky's ideas to take root was the need for a universal tank to fight this kind of war. Soviet weapons makers had been working on advanced designs for some time, but in 1936 the man who comes as close as anyone at being the creator of the path-breaking T-34, Mikhail Koshkin, arrived at the Kharkov armaments center as head of the Tank Design Bureau. Koshkin was brilliant in his own right, but he also put together a superb team of experts, men like A. A. Morozov, in charge of power train, who invented the best tank engine of the war; and M. I. Tarshinov, creator of the all-important hull configuration of the T-34, arguably the single most important step in the history of tank design, as we shall see shortly.

Most important of all, Koshkin clearly understood what he was about, the design and creation of the first all-purpose tank, unlike anything else in the world, a general model of tank that would perform superbly in all roles, simplifying tactics and especially production to a degree unprecedented. In August 1938, speaking before the High War Council, led by Chief of Staff Klementi Voroshilov, but with Stalin present, Koshkin nevertheless refused to mince words and spoke his mind. He called for the production of his personal project, arguing, "it is a kind of universal vehicle . . . It is superior to the light tanks in armor and armament, to the medium tanks in armament, and the heavy tanks in speed and maneuverability. . . . It can be used as a penetration and support tank for the infantry as well as for independent operative actions." This speech won the day, work continued, and the T-34 was first put into the field in September 1940, shortly after which, Koshkin tragically died of pneumonia brought on by overwork.

His masterpiece, however, made all the difference in the war. Every authority agrees that the T-34 was the most important tank of World War II, and, in fact, one of the few designs to change the entire nature of armored design.[12] Let's take a look at what all the fuss is about, first by looking at the various components, then summing up the whole design and its significance.

T-34

We begin with armor, for that is where the T-34 has made the biggest contribution. Prior to its introduction, all tanks used a stepped approach, somewhat like layers on a wedding cake, or like setbacks on an office building. At the base was the hull, with the driver seated inside, surmounted by a superstructure, then topped by a turret; all of these were constructed from vertical or near-vertical plates, as with the Mk III or Mk IV being typical.

The Soviet team, instead, introduced the principle of sloped armor that every tank has used ever since. This is another one of those ideas that seems so logical, so simple, it is hard to believe that no one had used it before, but that is always true of the really great inventions.

Sloped armor has a number of advantages that remain as true today as they did in 1940. One of them is that it provides shot-deflection, the possibility that a shell might ricochet off, although as anti-tank shells increased in velocity, that became less and less likely. Far more important, however, is that they increase the relative depth of the armor, by presenting a longer path for any oncoming projectile to penetrate; the smaller the angle from the horizontal, the better. This is limited, of course, by just how little room you want to give the driver and the men in the turret; no one can construct an entirely horizontal hull, although modern battle tanks like the M1 Abrams, which places the driver in a severely reclining seat, have come as close as possible. In World War II, about the best that anyone could do was an extreme 30 degree angle off of the straight horizontal, which effectively doubled the thickness of the armor to an oncoming anti-tank round.

That, in fact, was just what the T-34 designers did. They created a glacis plate 45 mm thick (1.8 inches), but set it at 32 degrees, so that it had the thickness of roughly 90 mm (3.6 inches) when struck by an oncoming shell. The sides were much less, the same 45 mm but sloping at 49 degrees; nevertheless, this was still better than the slabsided German tanks of that era achieved. Similarly, the turret front was more rounded than that of anything in the Wehrmacht's arsenal, and while the original model had 45 mm protection, by the last model (produced in 1943) this had gone up to 70 mm. This was also of solid quality, by the way; writers are still commenting that the Russian armor was inferior to that of the West, but an inspection of the T-34 Model 1942 by the British School of Tank Technology revealed that Soviet armor plate was equal or better than that being fielded by the Brits. Their involvement also points to just how far ahead the Russians really were; the *first* British tank to have a sloped glacis (or front plate) was the

Centurion, which did not appear until mid-1945, so far at the end of the war that it did not see service in that conflict (although it was one of the premier tanks of the Cold War).

If the T-34 revolutionized the design of armor, it also led the way when it came to firepower. As noted earlier, the Germans used a high velocity 37 mm or 50 mm gun for tank warfare, and a short-barreled 75 mm for destroying fortifications with high explosives. The Russians, however, went them one better, by mounting a 76.2 mm cannon, originally only L/30.5, but by 1941 this had been replaced by an L/42, high-velocity version that was superior to any other gun mounted on any tank in the world at that moment. It could outshoot anything the Germans had in a tank, and outshone French and British guns as well. The standard armor-piercing shell in 1941 could punch through 69 mm of armor at 500 meters (more than anything the Germans had on a tank at that point), 61 mm at 1,000 meters, and even 48 mm at 2,000 meters, making possible a successful hit on side armor at long range, although there were very, very few Russian crews capable of that kind of accuracy. By 1943, however, they were also fielding a sub-caliber Arrowhead round with a tungsten core penetrator, capable of penetrating 92 mm of armor at 500 meters.

In addition to this, the 76.2 mm also carried formidable high-explosive and fragmentation rounds, both weighing over 13 pounds and capable of solid destruction to structures and soldiers. Thus, the original T-34s carried seventy-seven rounds (although this went up to one hundred rounds by the 1943 version), consisting of nineteen armor piercing, fifty-three high explosive, and five of shrapnel. In 1941, when the Germans launched their invasion of Russia, no other tank had that kind of capability.

The third part of our original triumvirate of tank characteristics was speed, and the T-34 set strides here as well. Back in 1928 an eccentric American named Walter Christie came up with a novel suspension that permitted tanks to travel at very fast speeds. Christie, from all accounts, was at best idiosyncratic, in moderation irascible, and in extremes a major pain in the keister to get along with, so it is not surprising that the buttoned-up types in the U.S. Army did not get along with him.

Which was really petty and stupid, because Christie was also a genius. His design mounted a few large road wheels on pivoting lever arms which rode on immense coiled springs that permitted enormous vertical movement. The result was a high degree of deflection, the ability to withstand and buffer extremes of ground and contour without undue suffering to the crew.

This system, however, which the Russians bought and then implemented for their medium tanks, provided much more than the ability to successfully traverse terrain that would bounce crews in every other nation's tanks into the turret roof. More important, it meant that the Russian tanks could now move faster as well, because the shock caused by this greater speed was cushioned.

At this time, most main tanks moved in the 20 to 25 mph range, including the emergent American Sherman. If one looked at infantry tanks, however, and heavy tanks in general, this could drop considerably, to as low as 8 to 10 mph.

The T-34, on the other hand, could move out at 34 mph. That may not seem like much to the driver of a modern automobile that cruises at 70 mph, but to someone trying to line his sights onto a fast moving tank, it made a deuce of a lot of difference. Writer Richard Humble, for example, told how he "still cherishes the salty comments of an . . . 88mm gunner trying to explain the stark terror of being at the business end of the best anti-tank gun in service, while at the same time being virtually unable to draw a bead on T-34s advancing flat-out across country."[13]

This kind of speed was also possible because of the superb engine the Russians had developed. Despite the fact that the Germans were the acknowledged masters of diesel engines, they were extremely late in designing power plants of this sort for tanks, relying instead on gasoline engines, as did the Americans. Instead, the Russians jumped way ahead, designing the V-2, a 12 cylinder, 38.9

liter engine capable of 500 horsepower (hp) at 1,800 rpm, with work beginning in 1932, when German industry had not even started to experiment with diesels for tanks. This pioneering power plant, made out of aluminum, no less, was so good that it not only powered most of the World War II vehicles, but in later, improved versions, continued to be built in the 1970s for tanks as sophisticated as the T-62 series.

The V-2 diesel gave the Russians a number of critical advantages, including, as most motorists know, that diesel fuel costs less than gas. More important was the simple fact that it also does not catch fire nearly as readily as gasoline does, a somewhat relevant issue if you happen to be inside one of these vehicles when it gets hit. Germans used to refer to gasoline-engined Shermans as "Ronsons," claiming that, like the cigarette lighter of that name, all you had to do was strike them in order to make a flame go up.

But the fact that diesel fuel burns slower than gasoline also provided the Russian tanks like the T-34 with incredible range. The German Mark IV could cover less than 100 miles on a tankful, while the Tiger was extremely limited in its ability to fight a fast moving battle, having to refuel after a minimal 60 miles. The T-34 on the other hand, with fuel tanks wedged in the sides beneath the armor, plus a series of external drums that were standard features, could cover 280 miles before the gauge read "empty," offering a capacity for long-range operations that no enemy tank could match.[14]

There were other automotive aspects of this tank that made it stand out as well. The relatively powerful engine gave the T-34 one of the best power-to-weight ratios in the world, a critical factor in determining just how effective a tank can be and how much power is available to the driver regardless of the relative weight of the vehicle. Mk IIIs and IVs had a ratio of around 15.5 hp per ton (depending on the model), in the Tiger this dropped to 13 hp/ton, and in the Panther it was 16 hp/ton. The T-34, on the other hand, had 17.9 hp/ton, and the only tank that came close to that was the American M4 Sherman, with 16.9 hp/ton, which did not appear until a year or two after the T-34. Just to put this into perspective, the American M18 tank destroyer, until the advent of the M1 Abrams, the fastest armored vehicle in history with a top speed of 55 mph, had a ratio of only 20.5 hp/ton.

This power was coupled with extremely wide tracks, which provided the T-34 with very low ground pressure; the lower the pressure, the less likely that a tank will sink into the mud or snow. At a time when German tanks had treads not much wider than one foot, the T-34s covered nineteen inches of ground across their entire length. As a result, their ground pressure was much lower, compared to other vehicles: whereas the Mk III rated 13 to 15 pounds per square inch (depending on model), the Mk IV had 10.6 lbs/sq.in., the Tiger came in with a tank sinking 15 lbs/sq.in., the more maneuverable Panther reached 12.5 lbs/sq.in., and the Sherman back up to 14.3 lbs/sq.in. The T-34, on the other hand, rode around with an incredible pressure of only 9.1 lbs/sq.in.

These numbers meant that the Russian tanks could go where other tanks could not. In the Russian winters and subsequent muddy seasons the T-34s were unstoppable, maneuvering with their wide treads when the German machines were bogged down everywhere; the Germans called them "Snow Kings," and with good reason. Russian tanks, for example, could cruise through snow three feet deep; as late as February 1947, in Task Force Frigid Exercise, American M26 Pershing tanks overheated their engines in thirty inches of light snow.[15]

There were other little automotive advantages as well. If, in the middle of a terrible Russian winter the engine would not turn over, the driver could always use the compressed air stored in cylinders in the front of this tank for this purpose, a feature no other tank had, but which guaranteed that the tank would crank up despite freezing temperatures. In addition, the Russians put their transmission in the rear, instead of the front as in Western tanks; as a result, they eliminated the need to have a drive train run to the rear of the tank, opening up room in the main cabin.

And finally, the T-34 was capable of mass production, to an extent only challenged by the Sherman; even there, however, despite the enormous resources of the American automobile industry, more T-34s were made than any other tank in World War II. This will have much more importance, and will be described in more detail, later on.

BALANCE

When we started this discussion, we stated that what made a great tank was not any one characteristic, but balance. And that is what is so striking about the T-34. Other tanks had bigger guns or heavier armor, but few tanks have ever been as good a package as this. Whether or not the T-34 was the best tank in the war or not (we shall see), it was one of the best balanced of all time.

Walking around the T-34 confirms this fact. All the great weapons have always had a certain style about them, a grace that goes beyond their simple specifications, a beauty of line that just looks right. The Colt .45 Peacemaker is a supreme example of this, a gun that one knows is superb even before touching or firing it.

So it is with the T-34. When I first saw one and walked around it, the line that came to me was that used by sailors in the Rodgers and Hammerstein musical *South Pacific*, where they discuss a woman by observing where "she's narrow, she's as narrow as an arrow, but she's broad where a broad should be broad." Similarly, from the front and sides, the T-34 is a masterpiece of narrow lines, the sharp angle of the turret moving straight into the angle of the side armor, a solid wall designed to deflect shot. The turret sits there, small and difficult to line up in a crosshair. Yet, when you walk around to the rear it is all broad beam. What stands out here is the wide body of the tank and even more, the expansive treads, the visuals emphasizing just how maneuverable this tank was on ground that would swallow up anything else. Even its successor, the T-34/85—a much better tank by far—does not look this good, this right.

T-34 (photo by author, U.S. Army Ordnance Museum, Aberdeen Proving Ground)

T-34 (photo by author, U.S. Army Ordnance Museum, Aberdeen Proving Ground)

T-34 (photo by author, U.S. Army Ordnance Museum, Aberdeen Proving Ground)

THE T-34'S FLAWS

Not that the T-34 did not have flaws, because it had plenty. And that is ignoring the fact that creature comforts ranged from negligible to nonexistent, compared to Western tanks; Russian peasants had grown up in sufficient poverty, especially during the horrific food shortages of the Stalin years that killed millions, that they did not expect anything of the sort. One way to gain a handle on this difference is to note that whereas many Germans had experienced the luxury of riding in a motorcar, and America had the highest ratio of cars to person in the world by a remarkable margin, few Russians had ever been in an auto, so they had no expectation as to what kind of conditions motorized transport could or should offer.

But there were plenty of other problems, and they were both real and fundamental, factors that dramatically limited the T-34's effectiveness. That small turret, for example, such a restricted target for the enemy, was a nightmare to fight in. This only permitted a two-man crew (instead of three, as in Western tanks), which meant that the commander had to work as gunner too, severely limiting his ability to direct the tank in battle. In normal circumstances, the job of a commander is to maneuver his tank, point out targets and call for fire, and fight within a larger battle plan, all done effectively and with wisdom and skill. This is more than enough for any officer, and frequently above their talents at that. To add on the necessity to aim and fire the main armament creates a recipe for disaster, as neither the commander's function nor the gunner's gets done very well, if at all. When one recognizes that this was also the case for platoon and company leaders in their tanks—men with even greater command responsibilities since they fight the entire unit, as well as their own tank—the implications become drastic indeed.

That wasn't the only problem the commander had, although it was the worst. Right behind in the potential for fatal results was the fact that the T-34 had no 360 degree vision cupola like the German tanks did, equipped instead with only a narrow viewing slit and an even narrower periscope that could at least turn in its socket. This meant, however, that the only way the commander could work at all was by sticking his head out of the hatch, a tactic many tank commanders have adopted, but was practically a necessity with the T-34.

When the commander did stick his noggin out, the chances were pretty good that it would be shot off, too, because of another design flaw. The T-34, up until the later models, had a huge single-piece hatch that opened the wrong way; that is, the hinge was on the front, not the back. This may not seem like much, but it meant that, first of all, he could not just open the hatch a little and take a peek. Instead, the Russian officer had to pivot up this large piece of metal, which then obstructed his view and forced him to stand up all the way in the turret so he could see over it. Not a recipe for survival, not at all.

Add to this the fact that a Russian tank commander had no way of communicating with other tanks. Up until 1943 most Russian tanks did not have radios, which meant that the only way to talk to other tanks was by waving signal flags! Besides being slow and unreliable (i.e., hard to see amidst smoke and explosions), this was, of course, hardly what a tank commander, burdened with the requirements of being gunner as well, wanted to do in the midst of combat. There is also the small matter of what kind of target it made to have a man stand up in the turret and wave brightly colored pieces of cloth about; instead, commanders usually led by simple example, having the other tanks follow their lead in combat. This prevented the use of any kind of sophisticated tactics, and meant that the Russians had enormous difficulty dealing with the quick-response ideology built into blitzkrieg.

There were other flaws as well. The transmission may have been in the right place, but it was not all that reliable, as the Russians, despite their superiority in building rugged engines, never designed anything to match the German Maybach transmission. At the start of the war, the situation was so bad that Russian tanks could be seen going into battle with spare trannies strapped to their rear deck, and while it got better as the war progressed, the T-34 never enjoyed a really first-rate system for shifting gears.

On top of this, Russian tankers were woefully undertrained, with crews getting as little as seventy-two hours in the classroom after they had finished basic, and possibly even less in the worst periods of the war. This left little time for learning about the vehicle itself, and even less for exercises that taught how to operate within and coordinate with larger units.

The result was terrible battle performance in the first year or so of the war, compared to the enormous potential the T-34 offered (and later delivered). The Germans, notwithstanding their shock at discovering the quality of Russian war machines, noted how tank units fought in "a disorganized fashion with little coordination," that they tended "to clump together like a hen with its chicks, the less experienced tanks following the lead of the platoon or company commander."[16]

T-34/85

Besides all these problems, by 1943 the T-34 was being surpassed by newer German models like the Tiger and the Panther, so in 1943 it was redesigned. To start with, Russian designers implemented a much bigger turret, with a ring diameter of 5.2 feet. This meant that, finally, another crew member could be added, so that the turret could now operate with a separate commander, gunner, and loader. This alone added enormously to the tank's effectiveness in battle. In addition, the new turret's frontal armor was much thicker than that of its predecessor, 90 mm, or almost as much as a German Tiger had. And finally, radios were now standard issue, so the signal flags could finally be burned!

Another major change was in the gun. After considerable testing, the Russians decided to adopt an 85 mm anti-aircraft gun designed originally in the pre-war period, but available in large numbers and with far superior performance to the 76.2 mm. One indication of its effectiveness: as an antiaircraft weapon the 85 mm was still potent enough to give American flyers lots of trouble over the skies of Hanoi, two to three decades after the end of World War II.

This weapon, in its L/54.6 version, again fired high explosive and fragmentation rounds, although of a larger weight and hence, firepower than those of the 76.2 mm gun. It also carried as standard a much better anti-tank round, the BR-365, which could penetrate 111 mm of armor at 500 meters, 102 mm at 1,000 meters, and 85 mm at 1,500 meters, which meant it could tackle the front armor of the Tiger I. But by late 1944, penetrator munitions had been adapted to this size weapon, in the form of the BR-365P (P was short for *podkaliberniy*, or subcaliber). This round was somewhat inaccurate, so had limited use at long ranges, but at shorter distances was formidable; at 500 meters it could go through 138 mm of armor, or 5.5 inches. This gun also gave the tank its new name, and forever after this version would be referred to as the T-34/85, its predecessor as the T-34/76.

T-34/85 (photo by author, U.S. Army Ordnance Museum, Aberdeen Proving Ground)

T-34/85 (photo by author, U.S. Army Ordnance Museum, Aberdeen Proving Ground)

The first T-34/85s came off the production lines in December 1943, and by March 1944 were in the hands of Russian soldiers, especially in the elite Guards units, which always received the best equipment first. Soon production outpaced that of the T-34/76, as the new tank supplanted and then replaced it: in 1943 the Russians made 15,529 T-34/76s and only 283 T-34/85s, but by 1944 the figures had reversed, to 2,995 T-34/76s as opposed to 11,778 T-34/85s; by 1945 none of the smaller tanks were made anymore. At the time of its debut, it was by far the most powerful medium tank available to any of the Allies anywhere.

Hans Halberstadt is one of the few writers who, like Timothy Mullin, actually tests the weapons he talks about. His book, *Inside the Great Tanks*, reads like the ultimate fantasy for the rest of us, as he tells what it is actually like to drive everything from a World War II half-track to an M1 Abrams tank.[17]

Halberstadt's report on this weapon began on an iconoclastic note: the T-34/85 is a lot roomier than it is usually given credit for, and is in fact much more so than the American Sherman. This is despite the fact that the latter was more than three feet taller than the T-34/85 (and thus presented a much better target) and was supposed to have far more creature comforts than the spartan Soviets ever provided. Not so.

Driving it, on the other hand, fits the stereotype of weapons designed for the stolid Russian peasantry, at least at first. All the T-34s were notorious for having clutch and steering mechanisms that can only be referred to as "brutal," with all levers incredibly stiff, requiring enormous strength to use them. Halberstadt claimed, given both this incumbrance and the tightness of any tank's interior, that "the ideal driver for the tank is a guy who looks like a short linebacker."[18]

This smooths out some as the T-34 gets up to speed, but Halberstadt and his companions who helped with the testing had a number of other comments. While visibility is limited, the ride is quite good, due to the suspension and oversized tracks. The engine is "a great powerplant, very well designed and highly dependable." Comparing the tank overall to its counterpart among the Western allies, they state, "it's a much better design than the M4 Sherman, with a lower silhouette, much better gun, better armor, better slope, a great suspension system, simpler, easier to maintain— superior machine. . . . if they'd gone up against our American tanks at the time, we'd have lost." Overall, they referred to it as "simple, without frills, designed to fight and survive . . . a fast, reliable tank," with armor that "is thick and beautifully shaped." Through- out the decades of the Cold War, Soviet satellites and aligned coun- tries continued to use this durable design, and by the mid-1990s it was still in the armory of over thirty nations, albeit usually in a second-line capacity.[19]

The key to the T-34/85's greatness, above all, is again, simply balance; it is arguably the best-balanced tank in history. Because of this, the T-34 series becomes one of—some would say *the* pioneer— in that it was the tank that created the concept of the modern main battle tank MBT, one that could do most of what the lights, mediums, and heavies did before, and in one, easily standardized package. This is the setup every country looks to today when building or buying tanks, and has been since the end of the war, after the T-34 proved that one tank could do it all.

Just about every major tank writer has acknowledged this fact, the T-34/85's place in history. Steven Zaloga, who possibly knows more about Eastern Bloc armor than anyone else, at least among Western experts, says that the T-34 series "set the pace for world- wide tank development," while Bryan Perrett called it "the grand- father of all modern tank design," and Richard Humble flamboyantly—but accurately—remarked, "Since the German inva- sion of Russia . . . world tank development has never been the same." Some of the top writers go even further, with Christopher Chant saying it "was arguably the most influential tank ever devel- oped," and Chris Ellis and Peter Chamberlain called it "the great- est tank design in the history of armored warfare."[20]

I differ in my evaluation, but only slightly. I think that the T-34 is one of two tank series that sit in my Armor Hall of Fame; one consists of the original British tanks fielded in the Great War, that started this whole story, and introduced the world to armored warfare. Nothing could be more trendsetting than that.

But after that comes the T-34s. They created the MBT, both by their remarkable balance and by exceeding expectations in all the important areas, in armament, speed, and armor. In the last category, they introduced the critical design feature, sloped armor, that literally differentiates all tank shapes into pre- and post T-34. As I said before, this is the most *important* tank of the war, one of the most important in history.

But was it the best? There is no question that it introduced defining concepts, but could it really slug it out with the German heavies? We shall have to see. First, back to our story, starting with what happened when the German Army, with its Mark Is to IVs, invaded Russia and encountered the T-34 and its cousins.

10

GERMAN TANKS: FINAL GENERATIONS

TO PUT IT MILDLY, the new Russian tanks came as something of a surprise to the Germans. Infantry equipped with the standard 37 mm antitank cannon as well as panzer commanders in their Mk IIIs and IVs all started to send back horror stories after they encountered the T-34. The commander of one battery of guns told how "Half-a-dozen anti-tank guns fire at the T-34, which sound like a drum roll. But he drives through our lines like a prehistoric monster"; some units now took to calling their guns "door-knockers," because they could do little but clang on the heavy, well-sloped Russian armor. At the battle of Brody-Dubno, one T-34 shrugged off a seemingly unbelievable twenty-three rounds from a resolute, but frustrated and probably terrified 37 mm crew. Only on the twenty-fourth shot did they manage to jam the turret with a lucky shot, forcing the tank to retire. One Mk III officer reported how a teammate's tank "made hits on a T-34, once at about 20 meters[21] and four times at 50 meters . . . without having any noticeable effect. . . . The T-34s came nearer and nearer although they were constantly under fire. The projectiles did not penetrate but sprayed off the side." The divisional history of the Wehrmacht's Eighteenth

Armored Division quoted a lieutenant on his encounter with the Russian war machines, "Hauptmann [Captain] Kirn is firing madly . . . all his hits spray off their targets. The first T-34s. Terror is spreading among us." Another officer remarked, "Even using special ammunition we were not able to knock out these tanks." As one authority on German armor put it, "The confidence of the German infantry and anti-tank guns units was shattered utterly."[22]

Even worse were the heavy tanks the Russians had introduced, the KV series, which had armor 75 mm thick, far more than anything the Germans had ever experienced at that stage of the war. German antitank shells literally bounced off them at a range of fifty meters, and a single KV held up the advance of the entire Sixth Panzer Division for two days in June 1941. Impervious to enemy fire, it destroyed twelve trucks and a 50 mm gun brought up to deal with it, then knocked out an 88 mm cannon at 900 yards. Finally, while Mk IIIs with their 50 mm cannon made distracting suicide runs, an 88 mm was wheeled into position to take it from close in. Later investigation found that the 50 mm shells had hardly dented the armor, and of seven 88 mm rounds fired, only two penetrated; the finale came only when engineers dropped explosives into the turret. One German war correspondent captured the fear when he wrote of "[l]oud engine noise from all sides—clouds of dust rise up all around us. . . . And then the giant tank barrels rise from the horizon . . . a gigantic tank body. Tanks! Giant tanks such as we have never seen before!" Terrified, he continued to describe what combat was like on the Russian front, "Crippling fear falls over us. Then the antitank guns are called in; out of all their barrels fire roars, but their light . . . shells can do nothing here. Like rubber balls the shells bounce off the mighty steel walls. . . . The antitank soldiers fight wildly, as if possessed. . . . They fire until the armor plates glow from the . . . impacts . . . of the . . . shells. . . . [T]he last man sinks down over his gun."[23]

Beyond the strength of the armor, there was also the firepower of the Russian tanks, which was deadly to their German opponents. A tank officer reported, "Time and again our tanks have been split right open by direct frontal hits. The commander's cupolas on the PzKpfw III and PzKpfw IV have been completely blown off . . . proof of the great accuracy and penetration of the Russian T-34's 76.2mm gun." He complained, "The former pace and offensive spirit will evaporate and be replaced by a feeling of inferiority, since the crews know they can be knocked out by enemy tanks while they are still a great distance away." One panzer sergeant remarked, "Numbers—they don't mean much, we were used to it. But better machines, that's terrible. You race the engine, but she responds too slowly. The Russian tanks are so agile, at close range they will climb a slope or cross a piece of swamp faster than you can traverse the turret. And through the noise and the vibration you keep hearing the clang of shot against armor. When they got one of ours there is so often a deep, long explosion, a roar as the fuel burns, a roar too loud, thank God, to let us hear the cries of the crew."[24]

The Germans managed to achieve their tremendous victories in part because relatively few of the Russian tanks were the newer models, but mostly because Russian tactics were incredibly inept, while the panzer divisions performed superbly in direct combat. T-34s could deal serious blows in individual combat, but given these deficiencies, the overall effect was minor.

But the German generals knew what was happening, and took heed; the fact was, all their tanks, with the exception of the potential for the Mk IV, had been rendered obsolete in every category: armor, firepower, and speed. Guderian himself wrote, "Up to this time we had enjoyed tank superiority, but from now on the situation was reversed. The prospect of rapid, decisive victories was fading in consequence. I made a report on this situation, which for us was a new one, and sent it to the Army Group; in this . . . I described in detail the marked superiority of the T-34 to our Panzer IV and drew the relevant conclusions." He ended that document by insisting that "a commission be sent immediately to my sector of

the front and that it consist of representatives of the Army Ordnance Office, the Armaments Ministry, the tank designers and the
firms which build the tanks." Finally, he added, "The officers at
the front were of the opinion that the T-34 should simply be
copied, since this would be the quickest way of putting to rights
the most unhappy situation of the German Panzer troops."[25]

Guderian had enough clout that notwithstanding the Fuhrer's
optimism over the legitimately fabulous victories in the first
months of the Russian Front, the commission was formed straight
away. Officials came, looked over the enemy's weapons, and
despite the urging of many Panzer officers, rejected post haste the
idea of copying the T-34.

Though there is mixed opinion on this, there is no doubt in
my mind that the idea of duplicating a Soviet tank was never really
considered. The reason: racism, to use a word unfortunately appropriate to what went on in the East between 1941 and 1945. The
Germans fervently believed that Slavs were an inferior *race* (not
an ethnic or national group) and that offspring, for example, resulting from a mating between a Slav and a Teuton would be degener-
ate stock. Wehrmacht soldiers considered their invasion a war on
behalf of civilization, that is, they would bring the superior
German culture to these backward peoples and teach them to be
better. If not, they would kill all of them.

As a result, the war was fought with a barbarity on both sides
that Western Allies never experienced,[26] with no quarter asked nor
given. Soviet POWs died by the millions in German hands (among
other niceties, they removed all outer garments like top coats from
these prisoners, then left them in outside pens during a Russian
winter), and not many of those Germans who fell into Russian
hands made it through the war either. German units even exercised
this attitude—with fatal results—on large sectors of the Russian
populace that were prepared to move against Stalin, who instead
returned to Soviet service after suffering German atrocities.

These racial feelings also influenced the decision over what kind of tank to build; there was no way German officers and technicians could accept the idea that a Slavic machine was so much better than theirs. So instead of undertaking the most expedient solution of them all, and one technically feasible—basically copying the superior T-34—the Germans decided to design their own, new tanks, to counter the Russian technological threat. Thus started the major, and in fact the only arms race in tanks of the war, one that Western nations did not participate in until much later, but was always life and death in the East. In addition, it also caused the Germans to work on two of the finest tanks ever produced, the Tiger and then the Panther.

THE TIGER

Let me be very clear: the Panzer Mk VI Tiger is the single most *famous* tank of World War II, and was even back then, especially on the Western Front. Throughout the fighting in France, reports from American tankers seemed to constantly come back, "Tigers, Tigers," to the point that senior officers, who knew better, began to worry that GIs were coming to believe that the Germans didn't build anything but Tiger tanks. Even recently, when I contacted someone who sells T-shirts with tank pictures on them and asked about one with a T-34 or a Sherman on it (silly me), he said he only did the big German tanks because they sold so much better and noted that the Tiger shirts outsold everything else by a ratio of ten to one. Even worse, *Armor,* the official professional journal of the armored force in the United States, did an article on the great tank battle at Kursk for its March–April 2003 issue. At that time—July 1943—the total inventory of Tigers, operational or not, was only 262 machines, spread out over every theater, every front. So only a fraction of that small number wound up at Kursk, making them a very tiny part, indeed, of the 2,700 tanks and assault guns the Germans fielded there. Nevertheless, what did *Armor* put on its cover? Give you three guesses, and if "Tiger" doesn't come up first, you lose. You would think that at least these guys—real tankers—would know better. But it just reinforces the main point: at least in the West, *everyone* knows that the Tiger was the biggest, meanest, and toughest tank of the war. Or was it? And was it the best, both in the war and among German tanks?

Though the Germans had thought about the idea of a heavy tank for some time, its rapid development really took place in response to the new Russian threats. As early as 1937, the Henschel firm had received an order to develop what would be known as the Durchbruchwagen (DW), or "breakthrough tank." Progress went forward in a somewhat haphazard fashion, with designs started and then stopped and revised. In May 1941, even prior to the launch date of Barbarossa, Hitler met with top officials and gave orders to move more rapidly, in response to what they considered to be a growing threat from better quality British anti-tank guns.

After the Russian invasion, however, matters accelerated rapidly. Even Tom Jentz and Hilary Doyle, who have spent more time in the Tiger archives (and in the few remaining Tigers themselves) than anybody else, and who are at pains to claim that it was not just the Russian front fears that led to the Tiger, have to admit that after the start of that epochal campaign, "the design and production of an effective heavy Panzer was pursued with increased urgency." They also point out that the Tiger "was not created by following the standard practice of controlled design projects that were defined by careful implementation of a systemic series of conceptual design stages," but rather that it "came into being as a rush job." German tank scholar Wolfgang Fleischer also notes that "this tank was a makeshift solution in almost every way." By late 1942, the first vehicles were entering combat around Leningrad.[27]

We will come back to that design process, and the ideas behind the Tiger itself, in a few moments, but first let's take a look at the beast itself. It is a formidable one.

Panzer Mk VI Tiger (Thomas M. Tencza)

Tiger! The very name conjures up images synonymous with the notion of "tank," images of sheer, raw power, a tank that then, and now, symbolized armored might.

The Tiger made its reputation, more than anything else, on survivability and brute firepower. Most assuredly, it was heavy—60 tons, compared to the T-34/85's 31.5 tons and the Sherman's 30 tons—and for good reason. Frontal armor was an astounding 100 mm (3.94 inches), while the mantelet protecting the gun was even thicker than that, at 110 mm! This was so thick, that when the first British ordnance experts showed up to take stock of their new opponent, they did not have instruments big enough to measure armor of this depth. Even the side armor was 80 mm, more than the *primary frontal* armor of most tanks in the world at that time, and because of problems with rigidity caused by weight and the recoil from the large gun, the structure employed the largest one-piece armor plates possible. The entire sides and rear of the turret, for example, consisted of a single massive slab of armor bent into a horseshoe shape.

This made it an extremely difficult tank to kill, to say the least, given the firepower available at the time of its introduction.

The original Shermans all had a 75 mm gun, which could not penetrate the front or mantelet armor of the Tiger at literally point-blank range (a rather unenviable position to be in anyway, let alone with a gun that fails!), nor could the 76.2 mm of the original T-34s. The later U.S. tanks armed with the upgraded 76 mm high-velocity guns had a chance at very close ranges, but not a single one of the American tanks that came ashore at Normandy on June 6, 1944 carried that kind of weapon.

Meanwhile, the Tiger had an 88 mm L/56 derived from the famous FLAK 36 anti-aircraft gun that could reach out and touch at quite a long distance. British tests on the Tiger, using the standard armor-piecing round, discovered that the Germans could penetrate 102 mm of armor angled at 30 degrees at 1,000 yards, and 80 mm, much thicker than the frontal armor of the Sherman, at 2,500 yards. Basically, at the midpoint of the war, the Tiger could destroy most Allied tanks long, long before it could be penetrated. The gun itself weighed 1.31 tons.

One problem with the Tiger was the turret traverse; it was a hydraulic system that worked only when the engine was on, and usually gunners used a hand system that involved 270 turns of the wheel to travel 360 degrees. One English soldier told how he saw a Tiger trying to kill a small British tank, "but the turret of the Tiger . . . couldn't get . . . around fast enough," so that the smaller vehicle was able to fire a round into the German's lightly protected rear, and destroyed its seemingly superior opponent.

But this was countered by some other qualities, like the fact that the Tiger's weight made it an extremely stable gun platform. The British found that after they had sighted in the 88 mm cannon for a direct hit at 1,100 yards, the next five rounds—all fired without moving any of the controls—traveled straight to the target as well, despite recoil stress. In addition, the Tiger, like all German equipment from field glasses to submarines, enjoyed the fruits of the finest optics industry in the world. This enabled German commanders to literally *see* enemy tanks before they could be seen. One German gunner claimed that you could spot a blade of grass a mile away using the Tiger's sights, and an American officer writing a report after the war also noted how German sights have "more magnifying power and clearness than our own," which may not have been grammatical, but most definitely was accurate.

The introduction of the Tiger was not, however, all that auspicious; in fact it was downright disastrous. An initial detachment of four vehicles reached the town of Mga (southeast of Leningrad) on August 29, 1942, and by 11:00 A.M. were moving into battle.

Nobody at that time realized just how heavy the Tiger really was, and how much of a liability as well as an asset this could be, so no one checked out the boggy terrain, which caused the new tanks considerable difficulty. At the same time, the Tigers, which had been rushed into combat before all the bugs had been tested out, were extremely prone to breakdowns, so in a short while three out of four had been brought to a halt without any effort on the part of the Russians.

By mid-September, they had been repaired, and joined a new attack on the 22. This time the unit's commander, Major Richard Maerker, made a successful reconnaissance and recommended that the Tigers not be used, as the land was far too muddy. Hitler, however, personally wanted to see his wonder weapons in action, and countermanded that request.

Just past the start line, the first tank got hit in the front plate; the thick armor stopped the round, but the mechanical difficulties persisted, as the engine, rattled by the jarring shock of fast moving steel on plate, decided to shut down and would not start up again.

The other three tanks did better—for a while. On the attack, they were soon either knocked out by enemy fire or helplessly mired in the mud. With enormous difficulty, all but one of the Tigers was brought back to German lines, but the fourth was so deep in the ooze that nothing could get it out. Instead, a team of mechanics removed whatever they could, then stuffed the wreck with explosives and blew it to high heaven.

Tigers were always prone to mechanical problems throughout their lifetime, but they soon began to show what they were capable of. One Russian tank force, which had planned to deal with the Mk IIIs and IVs at a range of 1,250 meters, found itself surprised by the massive newcomers; two Tigers quickly knocked out sixteen T-34s, and as the Russians fled the scene of battle, the Tigers pursued and destroyed eighteen more. Some of the large 88 mm shells hit with such impact that they literally tore the turrets off the Russian tanks, and German soldiers began to joke that the T-34 lifts its hat whenever it meets a Tiger.

But the Tiger was far more effective on the Western Front than in the East. Part of this was the fact that the Russians eventually developed tanks that could handle the Tiger (see section on Heavy Tanks), while neither the Americans nor the British ever did, at least until the very end of the war (see section on the Sherman). Some of this resulted from the terrain; the Tiger always performed worst on soft soil, which meant that the Russian mud stopped it much more effectively than did French fields. But above all, the Tiger, with its slow speed and ponderous movement, was never a good weapon of blitzkrieg, but excelled in the kind of defensive warfare the Germans fought in Western Europe.

Tigers were stunningly effective, for example, at ambushes. The epitome of this came on June 13, 1944, in an incident that has now passed into legend, involving SS Lieutenant Michael Wittmann, the most skilled tank commander in history. That day Wittmann was carrying on a reconnaissance in his Tiger, when he came upon the Twenty-second Brigade of the British Seventh Armored Division (the Desert Rats of North African fame, no less). With the British stopped for tea, Wittmann and the other four tanks under his command cut behind them and proceeded to decimate the English unit. Within two minutes, Wittmann showed his prowess by having his own vehicle single-handedly dispatch *twelve* of the enemy tanks, and by the time his other four, now joined by eight more Tigers from another unit, had entered the fray, still another eighteen Allied vehicles were up in smoke. Later, the Germans retreated into the village of Vilers-Bocage, where fire from British tanks and anti-tank guns managed to at least stop Wittman's tank, even if they did not destroy it. Eventually, 4 Tigers would be done in, but a force of only 13 of these heavies had held up an entire brigade, knocked out 48 vehicles, and caused 255 casualties. Wittman, by the way, died two months later, his score in the Tiger by then up to 138 tanks and assault vehicles and 132 anti-tank guns destroyed by this superior commander of this remarkable vehicle.

Sounds like a war winner, doesn't it?

The Flaws of the Tiger

Not really. Don't get me wrong; the Tiger was a devastating tank, but there are some fundamental criticisms that must also be cited, ones that shape any evaluation of this tank.

Take the design, for example. It was strictly, positively retro, a slabsided layout that looked to the past and was not part of the future. The German designers needed something in a hurry, so they took the outdated layout of the Mk IV and built it up enormously. The armor plates on the Tiger, for example, for all their thickness, were laid out straight or near-straight vertical, bypassing any possible benefit from either shot deflection or increasing their depth to oncoming shot because of angling. Basically, the Tiger, also known as the Panzer Mk VI, was nothing new or at all innovative; it was simply a Mk IV, only bigger. That was why, by the way, Americans always thought they saw Tigers; at a distance, when differences in size disappear much quicker than differences in shape, the Tiger and the Mk IV became look-alikes. Roger Ford wrote that the lack of anything but 90 degree angles, the sheer vertical walls, "defines the essential character of the Tiger, and also . . . betrays the haste with which its form was defined. . . . It is difficult to understand why . . . designers came up with what is essentially a square box for the Tiger's hull."[28]

The real story of the Tiger, in other words, comes down to this: the Germans were shocked when what they perceived as the racially inferior Russians beat them in the tank race, and they went nuts as a result. Basically, they took the best existing tank they had, and practically in a frenzy, built it up massively, more than they needed. As Andrew Hull, David Markov, and Steven Zaloga so aptly put it, "the Tiger was a wild over-reaction to the tank panic that had set in after the first encounter with Soviet T-34 and KV tanks in the summer of 1941."[29]

So the Germans wanted something huge, and wanted it fast, but they paid a high price for those qualities. Severely limited production was one part of that bill, but the other was lousy mobility and lousy availability.

How lousy? The answer is: lots. Like a big bully with a fat gut, the Tiger was badly overweight, which made for a host of problems. First, it was slow, which meant mobile warfare, fast attacks, were out; and second it had extremely limited range. Allied troops were amazed that this monster could only run for a couple of hours before refueling, and that was on good roads; at its best, the Tiger had a range of only sixty miles. One German infantryman who fought in the hell of the Russian front wrote, "I was always very happy to see our tanks, especially the Tigers. The only problem was their very short range, which meant they would always leave us when we needed them the most. . . . I always preferred the support of our *Sturmgeschutz* (assault guns) who almost always stayed with us." In essence, the Tiger was an admission of defeat, a rejection of the fast-moving blitzkrieg tactics that had led the Germans to victory, and that were now being practiced by the Russians and even more, the Americans, the most highly mobilized force in the world.[30]

Weight carried other burdens as well, ones that nullified any hope of real mobility. All those extra tons put enormous stress on the engine, which caused breakdowns; to be really effective, the Tiger required a great deal of first-rate maintenance, much more so than the simpler and better designed mechanicals of the T-34 or Sherman; both of which needed far less support both in terms of amount and quality, which were not always available in the heat of war. One estimate claims that Tiger units lost 50 percent of their strength to breakdowns after two or three days in combat, and that this was halved again three days later. Another study of German tank losses on the Western front, found that, to quote scholar Erik Lund, "In the end, the Tiger was killed by its own operational mobility, which caused the Germans to abandon large numbers of their heavy tanks due to . . . mechanized casualties."[31]

Put more bluntly, the Tiger was not a reliable tank. On June 15, 1944, I SS Panzer Corps had thirty Tigers awaiting short-term repair, eight requiring major servicing, and *none* ready for combat. Ten days later, an SS unit with twenty-eight Tigers reported that twenty-five of them were in the shop.

Off-road travel was also a difficult thing, and had to be carefully planned to see if the soil could hold the huge weight of a Tiger; the tank had two kinds of treads: a wider set for difficult terrain, and a narrow set for railroad transport. The former were just over twenty-eight inches wide, dwarfing those of most tanks, but still giving a relatively high ground pressure of 15 lbs/sq.in. If the thinner, twenty-inch tracks were on, however, this went up to over 20 lbs/sq.in., which meant that it would be all too easy to sink the beast in anything but good roads and firm earth. In addition, bridges had to be reinforced, another cost imposed by the tonnage, paid for in delays and resources of men and material that could have been used elsewhere. Add to that the fact that the overlapping road wheels could get clogged with mud more easily than any other kind, and that the Russians would wait until they were solidly packed and frozen before they attacked, and this becomes a tank with a lot of downsides as well as assets.

Not a tank with balance, in other words.

So if the Tiger was not really a masterpiece, what was? The Panther.

THE PANTHER

There had always been two tanks planned to deal with the Russian tank threat Germany faced in 1941, and the Tiger was always seen as the more immediate response. At the same time, work went ahead on another design, one that would take more time and incorporate the Russian innovations.

Work on this version—the real, long-term German answer to the T-34—actually began before that of the improvised Tiger, so the Panther is enumerated as the Mk V, even though it had a longer developmental period and entered service after the Mk VI Tiger. Not very clear, but it was what happened.

That long development time, however, paid off, and the result was a superlative weapon of war, one of the true masterpieces of World War II armaments. Let's start this discussion by analyzing the armor, as this enables us to physically view the overall product and get a sense of what it was about.

In visual terms, the Panther looks like a Teutonic version of the T-34. It has the same sloped armor, the same harmony of line as the turret angle continues effortlessly into that of the hull. But there are no curves at all, no flowing lines, just hard angles, with stolid, heavy slabs of powerful armor everywhere. It is a blunt, fearsome killing machine, exuding brute strength; Hans Halberstadt calls it a "T-34 in drag," but there is nothing gaudy or frivolous about it.[32]

That visual impression is right on the nose, however, as the Panther was extremely well-protected, on a par with the Tiger. The front glacis plate was 80 mm thick, but unlike the vertical slab on its heavier cousin, this one was angled at 55 degrees, which gave it significantly increased protection and provided deflection as well.[33]

Panzer Mk V Panther (photo by author,
U.S. Army Ordnance Museum, Aberdeen Proving Ground)

Panzer Mk V Panther (photo by author,
U.S. Army Ordnance Museum, Aberdeen Proving Ground)

Guarding the turret was a frontal armor of 100 to 110 mm of steel (depending on the Panther model), with 45 mm on the sides, sloping at 65 degrees.[34]

What all this meant was that the Panther was invulnerable to most Allied guns if it was hit in the front. After landing in Normandy and confronting these beasts, the U.S. First Army became determined to see what would stop them. Accordingly, they put a captured Panther in the middle of a field and fired everything from rifle grenades to howitzer shells at it. Afterward, they found that their three-inch gun (the equivalent of the 76 mm gun on the upgraded Sherman) could only penetrate the front at under 200 yards, and the standard Sherman 75 mm had almost no hope at all. They claimed that at least the 90 mm could do the job at 600 yards, but later accounts say that M36 tank destroyers equipped with that gun could achieve these results only half the time, at ranges from 150 to 300 yards.

This was not such a good thing for the Americans, because if the Panther's armor was superb, the main gun was even better, arguably the strongest aspect of the entire design. Hitler had insisted on a better weapon than was in service on the improved Mk IV, the best German tank at the time the Panther was under development, and the Rheinmetall-Borsig company came up with an extremely long 75 mm gun, in L/70 caliber.

This gun may not have had the charisma of the 88 mm on the Tiger, but in truth, it was a better tank killer by far. The tremendous length of the gun enabled German munitions experts to devise a shell with an upgraded charge,[35] and the thinner profile of the 75 mm round (as opposed to the 88 mm) meant it had superior aerodynamic qualities and would suffer less resistance in the air.

The result was a very, very fast anti-armor round, with some of the best penetration of any gun of the war. Using the standard armor-piecing projectile, the Panther could go through 111 mm of plate at 1,000 meters and 124 mm at 500 meters, enough to decimate Shermans and even upgraded T-34s. If the crew had access to the extremely rare tungsten-cored armor-piercing round, however, this went up to 149 mm of penetration at 1,000 meters and 174 mm at 500 meters, or the ability to penetrate 7 inches of raw steel armor plate. One British tanker said that the Panther's 75 mm gun could open a Sherman easier than an infantryman could pry open a can of beans with a bayonet, hardly a comforting analogy.

This velocity also meant that the gun had superb accuracy. In its debut at Kursk, the Panther killed a T-34/76 at over 3,000 meters, a remarkable shot.* Controlled tests showed that it could hit a 2- by 2.5-meter target 100 percent of the time at up to 1,500 meters, dropping to only 92 percent at 2,000 meters. Basically, what all this meant was that, simply put, the Panther emerged as a supreme tank killer, capable of hitting Allied tanks long before they could get close enough for a killing blow. With that incredible 75 mm gun, it could stand off and wallop the dickens out of Shermans and even T-34s at 2,000 meters, while their shells bounced off its relatively thick and well-sloped armor. The only chance Allied tankers had was to either try and survive till they got to a range where their own guns were effective, or maneuver around to the sides or rear. Mechanically, the Panther was not bad either. A bit heavy (it was supposed to weigh 35 tons, but wound up tipping the scales at 45 tons instead), it had a first rate 700 hp engine and a solid speed of 28 mph on good roads.

Like the Tiger, the Panther did not make a good show for itself on first appearance, but became a formidable performer as the bugs got cleaned out. Hitler wanted to see how this new wonder weapon would do and insisted on using it at Kursk, in what was shaping up as the biggest tank battle of the war. Unfortunately, the first examples had not even undergone final testing and were hardly ready for baptism in battle. As a result, there were massive breakdowns all along the way, mostly because of transmission problems, while the engine, originally designed for a lighter tank, was also prone to overheating and catching fire. By the end of the first day, of the

---

*This is almost two miles. If you don't think that's far, find an automobile, walk or drive two miles away, and then take a look at it. Try to imagine hitting it with a bulky weapon with minimal vision and only in the hood (to replicate a turret or frontal shot).

184 Panthers that started out only 40 were left, most of the rest lost to mechanical problems and not enemy fire; many had broken down between the railway terminal and the front line, and didn't see any action. Three days later, only ten were still operational.

An awful lot of those problems got fixed on later models, and what was left was a supreme fighting machine, one that the other side was hard pressed to deal with. Noted author John Ellis quoted a commander of a unit of British Churchill tanks in a conversation that summed this up brilliantly. The commander had been asked what tank the Germans had most of, and he replied, "Panthers. The Panther can slice through a Churchill like butter from a mile away."

Hmmm. Not good. How does a Churchill kill a Panther then? "It creeps up on it," he replied. "When it reaches close quarters, the gunner tries to bounce a shot off the underside of the Panther's gun mantelet. If he's lucky, it goes through a piece of thin armor above the driver's head." Not exactly, shall we say, the kind of shot one would like to stake one's life on!

Nor the interviewer, obviously, who responded by asking if anyone had ever achieved this feat of arms. The answer: "Yes. Davis in 'C' Squadron. He's back with headquarters now trying to recover his nerve."*[36]

What made the Panther so great? A number of superior qualities— brilliant main armament, superb armor—but above all balance. Halberstadt called it "a complete package," and he was right; this tank had all the pieces, not just one or two, and they added up to a winner.[37]

---

*His description of Churchill versus Tiger, by the way, was even worse. The British officer claimed "a Tiger can get you from a mile and a half" and that the only way to reverse this was to get to within 200 yards and "put a shot through the periscope"! No one had ever pulled that one off, however, which is really not much of a surprise.

11

WHICH WAS BEST?

IT IS NOW TIME for the final accounting, then the drumroll and the envelope, please.

Let's face it: there are really only two contenders for the top spot, the Panther and the T-34/85. How do they compare?

Pretty close, in fact. Both, for example, fulfill the prime requirement of balance, with first-rate qualities across the board. In visual terms, as well, both have a certain panache, a sense of flow, albeit with very different styles.

But what about the specs? Here it is time to go, as the boxing writers used to say, to the tale of the tape. We return, in other words, to our three basic categories: firepower, armor, and speed.

On the first score, the Panther wins, but not by a wide margin, and even that depends on the range. As cited before, the Panther's standard armor-piercing round could go through 124 mm at 500 meters, compared to 138 mm for the Russian subcaliber round. But beyond that relatively close distance the Soviet round lost accuracy rapidly, so at 1,000 meters or more, the Panther was a much better killer by far; as mentioned, it had a far better stand-off capacity than the T-34/85, or any other medium tank for that matter. Add to that the possibility a Panther *might* have a few rounds of the relatively rare tungsten cored round, which could penetrate

174 mm at 500 meters or 149 mm at 1,000 meters, and it is clear who the winner is in this category.

Moving on to armor, the Panther is also better, but again, it depends on where and how you look to determine if the margin is by a lot or a little. The two turrets, for example, are not that far apart, with the Panther presenting a front of 100 to 110 mm, compared to the T-34/85's 90 mm. Where the Panther really shines, however, is in its frontal hull plate, a formidable 80 mm, compared to the Russian tank's 45 mm, which while it had a better slope, was nowhere near enough of a factor to compensate for a difference this large. Once again, this factor facilitated the Panther's ability to survive and make a kill at long range.

And finally, speed. Most sources give the T-34/85 an advantage at 31 mph against the Panther's 28 mph, but the numbers are sufficiently close to basically be considered a draw.

There you have it. The winner is clearly the Panther. Roger Ford wrote, "In trying to evaluate the tanks of World War II, the Panther provides [a] . . . benchmark—a standard against which to judge all the rest." Simply put, it was the best tank of World War II.[38]

Or was it? Go back to our original criteria, and there was that pesky category of availability. On this score there is another story.

In order to analyze this factor, I want to look at three critical elements: reliability, range, and production. Regarding the first, the Panther's engineers never really worked out all the bugs, and several major systems remained extremely problematic, in comparison to the overall solid record of the T-34 series. Most of this stemmed from the excess weight: the tank had originally been designed at thirty-five instead of forty-five tons, which meant increased strain on the suspension. It also meant that a more powerful engine had to be installed, which, in turn stressed the transmission and caused problems in that component as well, especially in the reduction gears that connected to the all-important drive sprockets; they were just too small to handle the torque they had to transmit, and gave constant trouble.

As a result, the Panther was mechanically unreliable, with a constant need for complex maintenance; the tank actually required a *complete* overhaul every 600 miles, an unthinkable figure for a Russian or American tank, but which meant that the tank had to be shipped back to Germany. Both T-34/85s and Shermans, by contrast, required fewer and simpler maintenance and repairs, which were a lot more likely to be done in the field, with far quicker turn-around time than anything the Germans could manage.

Because of all this, there were a lot fewer Panthers in combat than there should have been, reducing drastically its effectiveness as a war weapon. Even Peter Gudgin, who claimed that "the Panther was arguably the best tank produced by any of the combatants in the Second World War," had to admit, "it turned out to be almost as unreliable as the Tiger."[39]

If factors like these kept an awful lot of Panthers out of battle, so did the engine. Like those of other German tanks, it used gasoline rather than diesel fuel, which meant that it was much more prone to catastrophic fires than the Russian vehicles were. But gasoline burns at a much faster rate inside the engine as well; this, in turn, limited the Panther's range to little more than 100 miles, a serious drawback. It meant the German tank had to stop, withdraw, and refuel much more often; even more important, it denied the Panther the ability to make a *strategic* difference, to engage in long range forays against the enemy.

The engine was also pretty fragile and burned out quickly, especially in comparison to the rugged, dependable Russian and American power plants. Average engine life was only about 600 miles; after that, a Panther had to stop and have its engine replaced, which took a nine-man crew eight hours to accomplish. The final drive was even worse, by the way: this wore out every 90 miles.

But the biggest shortcoming of all was production methods, for this was, indeed, a fatal error.

The German style was always to try and design, then manufacture, the most perfect weapon possible, regardless of cost in

money or resources. They would then follow up with endless modifications to make it even better, while at the same time working
on an even better concept, which would be brought out as soon as
possible after the last tank, regardless of how the first one was
doing on the battlefield. They had a tendency, in other words, to
produce gold-plated weapons in the search for perfection, whether
or not they were necessary for the job. In most cases, for example,
you can make a machine that reaches 90 percent of the specifications in only a fraction of the time and cost that it takes to reach
100 percent. One of the best lines anybody ever wrote about the
Panther was that "it was ... like using a Rolls Royce car for
ploughing a field"; it could accomplish the task, quite obviously,
but was a tremendous waste, "was too good for the task," as a
British armaments expert puts it.[40]

Over and over, across the board, poor design *for production*
was the Achilles' heel of the German armaments industry. German
engines, suspensions, and transmissions were made with the finest
attention to detail possible, and then perfectly finished. The Tiger,
for example, was arguably the highest quality tank ever produced,
a beautiful jewel that required precision tools of great size and
simply lavish engineering facilities. It also used a sophisticated
steering system in contrast to the simple clutch-and-brake of
Russian and American tanks; when in doubt, the Germans rarely
failed to introduce complexity into their designs, regardless of the
consequences.

The results were predictable: the Tiger took an astonishing
300,000 man-hours to build and cost 800,000 Reichmarks per tank.
In that amount of time workers could send two Panthers into
battle, and that amount of money bought three Messerschmidt 109
fighters. Initial production rates for the Panther were only twelve
a week, not exactly the kind of output that wins a total war. One
captured panzer commander groused that his tanks had all been
designed by watchmakers.

This predilection made for a number of nightmares, especially in terms of logistics. While the Americans basically fielded only one tank, the Russians two (the T-34 and some version of a heavy), the Germans were constantly developing and placing in the field new vehicles, one on top of the other. Even at the end of the war, there were six new tanks in preparation, ranging from a light one at 5 tons to a super-heavy of 140 tons. As late as 1944, Germany was still trying to build simultaneously 425 different kinds of aircraft, 151 models of truck and 150 diverse kinds of motorcycles for the war effort.

To put it very mildly, these endless modifications did not help the spare parts situation one bit, since all the different models had noninterchangeable specifications; each little piece had been designed and fitted, of course, in the best possible manner, for the best possible results on that particular machine. By Summer 1942 supplies of spare parts had become critical, and this situation never really changed during the war. Add to this the fact that production was geared toward new tanks and not spares, and you have a situation where in some Panzer units they had to send technical officers away from the front and back to the factories, on unauthorized trips, in order to dicker for whatever spares they could get via personal appeals!

But the worst aspect of this attitude was production. Keep in mind that the Third Reich felt women's place was at home making blond babies, and only 182,000 were ever employed in the desperate armaments industry. Instead, their place was taken by millions of slave laborers; in tank factories they reached 50 percent of the workforce, and over 800,000 foreign workers toiled in Berlin alone by 1943. Instead of the robust, enthusiastic Rosie the Riveter or her Russian counterpart, Germans used starving, recalcitrant victims of racial terrorism.[41]

And because these people were making an endless series of different and new machines, production became pitiful, with large runs an impossibility. The Panther may have been a brilliant tank, but its introduction required shutting down entire production lines and then extensive retooling, which was not required to nearly the same extent when the T-34 became the T-34/85.

So the tale of the tape in this category represents pretty much failure on the Germans' part. As formidable as the Tiger was, only 1,354 were made in the *entire war*, and most astonishing of all, only 650 got produced in arguably the most crucial year, 1943, the year of Kursk, the turning point on the Eastern Front. In 1943, however, the Russians produced 15,529 T-34/76s, and the next year they built 11,778 T-34/85s; at that point, the Russians were producing almost as many T-34/85s *in a month* as the Germans would turn out Tigers in the history of the whole Reich. By the time the Americans and British landed at Normandy, the number of Tigers in the field on all fronts reached a peak at 613, but as losses mounted and with no new production (the Tiger production line stopped totally in 1944, while the Mk IV production kept on until the end of the war), by the end of the year there were only twenty-three Tigers on the entire Western Front, and only *one* was available for the Ardennes offensive. Of course, by then the Germans had moved on and had fifty-two Tiger IIs available, but the flaws inherent in this approach were apparent. Ford states that because of the Tiger's complexity and cost, "It would never be more than an occasional player."[42]

The Panther production story, while not quite as desperate, still fits the same pattern. Almost 6,000 got made, but with all the mechanical difficulties, it was rare that more than 500 were on the front lines of the vast Russian Front at any one time, a negligible figure. This in comparison to total wartime production of the T-34s in both models of over 53,000, more than any other Allied tank of the war by far, even the ubiquitous Sherman.

So what does all this add up to?

The final verdict goes like this: on a one-to-one basis, with a single, perfectly running Panther against a T-34/85 in the same condition, the Panther was the best tank of the war, and in particular, was much more likely to pick the Russian tank off at a greater distance, for a variety of reasons including armament, optics, and training.

But the Panther's various and profound shortcomings in design, from lack of reliability to low production, limited enormously its ability to affect the outcome of a battle, let alone a war. In terms of being designed for availability, the T-34 series had it all over any German tank that fought in World War II.

When looked at in this light, instead, the strategic quality of the T-34/85, as opposed to the Panther's tactical superiority, rises in importance. If you wanted to win in mano a mano conflict, choose a Panther. If you wanted to win the war, stick with the T-34/85.

Hans Halberstadt wrote, "In any of the innumerable arguments which crop up among armor enthusiasts as to which was the best tank of World War II, the M4 Sherman and the Panzer V Panther will always have their advocates, but for *all-around performance* (my emphasis—RS), the author's vote for the blue ribbon has to go to the Soviet T-34." He went on to state, "Tanks are all about fire-power, protection and mobility; in its developed version the T-34 had a very powerful gun, heavy and excellently shaped armor, a first rate engine and drive train—and it simply blew the doors off the competition." Marsh Gelbart, another British tank scholar, wrote, "Personally, I believe that the late model T-34 was the finest tank in service anywhere from 1939–1945."[43]

I don't agree with that judgment totally at the intimate level, but as a weapon to triumph in the larger picture, the T-34/85 sits at the pinnacle, the top tank of World War II.

PART III

OTHER ARMORED
VEHICLES

12

HEAVY TANKS

ALTHOUGH MOST NATIONS began looking to the medium tank as their all-purpose weapons platform, the predecessor of the Main Battle Tank, a few were able to successfully develop larger vehicles as breakthrough tanks, massive machines that could breach any possible enemy fortifications. The leaders in this field were the Germans and the Russians.

We have already discussed the Tiger, so it seems appropriate to start with the much more substantial Tiger II, also known as the Royal Tiger or the Konigstiger (King Tiger). At first glance this looks like the single most impressive tank of the entire war, but it really isn't. Let's take a look at what made it so good, and then what made it so bad.

TIGER II

The Tiger II's nomenclature is actually inaccurate, since this was really a new design, and one that in truth was derived from the Panther, with its sloped armor, rather than the older, traditional Tiger I. I have always felt that the proper designation should have been King Panther, or Panther II.

What made the Tiger II legendary, however, was not its name but two other attributes: firepower and armor. Regarding the first, it incorporated the big cousin of the Tiger I's 88 mm gun L/56, in this case an L/71 version.

That's right, a longer caliber gun than even the Panther had, but in 88 mm. One way to put this into perspective is that the barrel alone was over nineteen feet long, or more than the length of the Mk III tank in total! It fired a 36.3-pound armor piercing round, compared to the 27.5-pound in the Tiger I. This left the tube at a sizzling 3,340 feet per second (fps), much better than the L/56's 2,657 fps.

This gave the Tiger II a virtually unparalleled ability to knock the stuffings out of *anything* on the battlefield at vast ranges. It could slice through a Sherman, for example, at 3,500 meters with ease, and a German report showed that a round from the extended barrel 88 mm could penetrate 165 mm of armor set at 30 degrees at 1,000 yards; this is 6.5 inches, thicker than the armor on a U.S. light cruiser. If the armor was straight vertical, this went up to 215 mm, or 8.6 inches.

And if the Tiger II could kill its enemies with ease, it was a daunting task to return the favor (albeit not impossible), because of the thick armor this new tank carried onto the battlefield. The turret front was 180 mm thick—7.5 inches—set at almost vertical,[1] while the glacis was 150 mm at a well sloped 50 degrees. Even the *floor* was constructed from plates 40 mm thick—more than the frontal armor of the early Mk IIIs and IVs—and the sides were made from 80 mm plates. This last figure meant, however, that a T-34/85 could penetrate this large target at 1,500 meters, if it could maneuver into the proper position to get a shot off.

If all this was true, if the Tiger II had so many superlatives, then why wasn't it the best tank of the war?

To put it mildly, the Tiger II was, in mechanical terms, a disaster, and a stupid idea to boot. I'll come to that part in a minute.

Let's start with the engine, which is an important part of the story. The Germans wanted to introduce this new tank so badly that they did not have time to produce a new engine, so they used the same power plant that went into the Panther, with the same horsepower. Overall, this was not a terribly good idea, given that the Panther weighed 45 tons and the Tiger II tipped the scales at a tad more, say 68 tons. Not surprisingly, performance dropped to the cellar, in a whole lot of ways.

Take mobility; the Tiger II could do over 20 mph on good roads, but was a mess once it got off them, barely managing more than 10 mph. It could not keep up with any kind of rolling attack, and often had to be left far behind; few bridges in all of Europe could handle concentrated weight this extreme, forcing numerous detours for river crossings.

The extra weight of this Tiger also meant that no width of track could do much to help its flotation, and it could easily get bogged down. This in turn was made even easier by—again—the poor engine, which in turn gave little power, relatively speaking to the tracks: the Tiger II had a power-to-weight ratio (hp to ton) of only 10.1, compared to 12.3 in the none-too-agile Tiger I, and 15.6 in the Panther, a much better vehicle overall. In the Battle of the Bulge, the Tiger II was supposed to be the indestructible tip of the spear and had been collected in the hardest hitting segment, Task Force Peiper, which led the attack. But Lt. Colonel Joachim Peiper knew his business, that the Ardennes had poor terrain, narrow roads, and heavy woods, so he put out front the more mobile Panthers and Mk IVs. The Tiger IIs, on the other hand, he relegated to the utmost rear of his column, with orders to keep up as best they could, which they could not do very well at all, and soon fell behind.

Other problems prevailed; although the Tiger II had a huge, 175 gallon tank, it used gasoline, and gulped it at a rate similar to that of the proverbial lost soul in the desert; on cross-country trips, it managed only 2.5 gallons a mile. Because of this, range was limited to as little as sixty-eight miles.

Most important of all, the extra weight meant that the

mechanical components were constantly overstressed (e.g., the engine had to run at full power almost all the time), with the obvious result that breakdowns became frequent, to say the least. Because of this factor, the Tiger II was far less reliable than the Tiger I, which won no awards in this category, either; the first five production models of the Tiger II had to be destroyed before they ever even saw an Allied soldier because they broke down so much.

The inability to include a more powerful engine, however, points to the biggest folly of them all, namely that the idea was ridiculous in the first place, and never should have been started.

Look at it this way: here the Germans had the Panther, the best one-on-one tank of the war, capable of stopping just about anything at long ranges, especially on the Western Front, and what do they do? They slow production down to introduce a behemoth that couldn't move very fast when it ran at all, at literally double the cost of the Panther. If the Americans, on the other hand, had a tank anywhere near as good as the Panther at that point in the war, they would have produced the hell out of it, run the assembly lines flat out like they did for the Sherman. Instead, the Germans interrupted that to build a grand total of only 489 Tiger IIs, bringing new complications to the logistics system as well, as a minor by-product. Go figure.

In my opinion, no heavy tank was all that great, as they were too ponderous for the emerging concepts of fast moving armored warfare, but the Russians got the balance as right as it could be done.

JS-II

When the Germans fielded the Tiger I prematurely, one of the most costly consequences of this was the fact that they were easy to capture, thus eliminating any kind of honeymoon when the new heavy tank was unknown and thus no tactics had been designed to defeat it. Even worse, it meant that the Russian armament industry was alerted to this new challenge, and began to prepare a response.

This is exactly what happened in January 1943, when Soviet forces acquired a Tiger only months after it had been introduced to the battlefield. Examination and testing of this vehicle gave weight to the arguments of Russian tank designers, who had been pushing for a while to move past Stalin's ruthless dedication to producing only one model each of medium and heavy tank, and to work on new, upgraded versions. Thus, they finally won the right to develop a replacement for the KV series; given that Russia was locked into a life-and-death struggle with the vast bulk of the Panzer armies at the time, with Kursk only six months away, these orders had considerable force behind them, and planning proceeded apace.

The first big decision the Russians had to make regarded the armament, for this was a tank designed to take on the German heavies and win. In the first models, they installed the 85 mm antiaircraft gun, but as plans were underway to put this in the upgraded T-34, designers accurately noted that the heavy tank of the Russian forces should have a punch commensurate with this strength, and moved on.

There were two choices, a 100 mm and a 122 mm. The 100 mm was actually the better of them, a gun optimized for anti-tank warfare that fired a smaller, more aerodynamic round at a much higher velocity, and thus was a superior weapon for penetrating armor. The problem was that this gun was just now being developed, and it was not clear if it would be perfected in time. Simultaneously, the ammunition was a new caliber for the Russians, and it would be a while before it could be stockpiled, far behind the timetable for the new Russian tank. So instead, they went with the far more plentiful 122 mm; the 100 mm would later be used in the SU-100 tank destroyer, and we will explore and evaluate its qualities when we get to that discussion later on.

The 122 mm D-25 gun as actually installed had a number of benefits, but also some drawbacks. With a length of L/43 and firing a 55-pound shell at 2,600 fps, it could punch a hole in 160 mm of vertical armor at 1,000 meters, while a Tiger I could only deal with

138 mm on a similarly angled sheet. In an early test against a captured Panther, at 1,500 meters the 122 mm round punched a hole through the thick frontal armor, kept going through the insides, and then came flying through the rear armor and out into the Russian countryside. Just in case that did not happen, the round also had a high explosive filler at the core, which meant that it hit like a sledgehammer; even when it could not penetrate a turret, it could usually knock it clean off the hull with that kind of terrible force. One Russian account claims that a tank equipped with this gun fired two rounds at German armored vehicles: the first shell hit an assault gun and it "literally fell apart," while the second penetrated not one, but two of these machines.[2]

What made this an even better idea was that the 122 mm gun also had a superior high explosive round. The Russians knew that combat was hardly a discreet matter and that it was foolish to assume that a tank would only engage other tanks (in fact, most of the shells fired by any tank are high explosive, not armor piercing; the Russians calculated that the JS-II fired 70 percent HE and only 30 percent anti-tank shells). Their weapon, therefore, fired a formidable 55-pound high-explosive round, compared to the miserly 9 pound one used in the Panther (only one-sixth as large), and the Tiger's still inferior 20 pound round.

The 122 mm D-25 only had one problem, but it was a significant one. Because of the sheer size of this round, it came in two pieces, the shell and the charge. This meant that the gun had a slow rate of fire—about two or three rounds per minute—and that only twenty-eight complete rounds would fit within the tank, a tiny fraction of what most other tanks carried, thus necessitating frequent rearmings.

By now the tank had been named the Josef Stalin-II (JS-II or IS-II, depending on which alphabet you use), which was probably a wise piece of sycophancy given the dictator's murderous habits toward his bureaucracies, and it received armor tantamount to its firepower. The front plate could reach as much as 160 mm at

JS-II (photo by author at Duxford, UK)

30 degrees, while the mantelet was 120 mm thick. All this in a design that had a first rate ballistic shape, able to deflect shells at least as well as the Panther or Tiger II, and far superior to the Tiger I. One JS-II shrugged off five hits from a long barreled 88 mm L/71 at 1,500 to 2,000 meters, and was only penetrated at 700 meters.

In mechanical terms, too, the JS-II proved itself the best of a ponderous breed. No heavy tank ever moved as fast as a medium, and none were ever expected to. The Russian model had a 600 hp version of their basic diesel, an engine which seemed adaptable to every possible circumstance. This permitted a solid speed of about 27 mph, and combat range was about 150 miles on good roads. However, the JS-II only weighed about forty-six tons—about as much as a Panther, not a Tiger, and that gave it a much better power-to-weight ratio and much lower ground pressure, vastly improving mobility.

Thus, the JS-II emerges as a reasonably well-rounded heavy tank, with solid armor, a hard-hitting gun, decent speed, and reliability. This, in turn, combined with ease of production, a Russian and American trademark, in comparison to German and British tanks, and by the end of the war 3,400 JS-IIs had been made. One way to evaluate this achievement is to note that Germany produced three different vehicles that used the long barreled 88 mm

L/71 gun: the Tiger II, and the Jagdpanther and Rhinoceros tank destroyers. Total production of all three combined was still only about 1,000 units.

In the field, the JS-II proved formidable. The first Guards heavy-tank regiments to be issued the new weapon formed in February 1944, and went into action near Korsun-Shevchenkovski. In this and in other battles, the JS-IIs would follow about 300 to 500 meters behind the T-34s, knocking out enemy tanks from longer range, although if particularly strong resistance ensued, they would move through the line of mediums to form a heavy spearpoint to crush the enemy. Its relatively fast speed, furthermore, suited Soviet battle tactics at that time, since the Russians were now on the offensive, one that would take them all the way to Berlin. The awkward German heavies, more suited to defense, would not have worked in this kind of environment, and the more mobile JS series provided the tactical strength *and* mobility for a powerful offensive thrust.

To the Germans, this new tank came as something of a shock. Their first reports, out of Korsun-Shevchenkovski, read, "Newest heavily armoured and very heavily armed tank (counterpart of the 'Tiger'); future standard type of hard tank, very hard to fight." Seventy-five millimeter shells from anything less than a Panther bounced off, and even then it was difficult; the JS-II could penetrate a Panther at 1,200 meters, while the Panther had to move up to 600 meters to do the same damage. Unable to move much faster than the Russian tank, this put the Panther at a terrible disadvantage, often a fatal one. In May 1944 in Romania, the SS Grossdeutschland Division had their Tigers open fire at 3,000 meters, a distance at which they had previously been able to destroy any Russian tank they could hit. Now, however, they watched as the shells ricocheted off, and the Tigers had to move up to 1,800 meters to score a kill. Their commanding officer, Hasso van Manteuffel—one of the best practitioners of tank combat in the war—wrote, "This encounter was shocking, as previously our 88 mm gun had destroyed Russian tanks without difficulty. Now the Tiger crews could destroy the enemy tanks only with the greatest difficulty and suffering heavy losses." He later said that the JS-II was the best tank he saw anywhere at any place or time in the war.[3]

JS-III

As an afterthought, we should also note that a later model in the JS series, the JS-III, while too late to see combat, set the pace for armor in the early Cold War. This version was thoroughly redesigned—some writers refer to it as revolutionary, especially in the layout of the hull and turret—although the engineers kept the JS's proven mechanical core, including the engine, suspension, and power train. Among the most striking elements of this new tank was the hull armor. The main front hull plates, besides being a massive 120 mm thick, were welded together to create a sharp-looking edge, a point, instead of a flat surface, the only one of its kind ever fielded in the history of tanks; the designer called it the "eagle's nose," but the name adopted by the troops was the "shchuka" or "pike" (actually the translation is "pike's nose"). Besides being one of the best shot deflectors ever designed, this gave the tank a most formidable appearance. Standing in front of one of these, facing down a gigantic steel wedge aimed right at you, remains a disconcerting experience even today.[4]

The turret, on the other hand, pioneered the low, flat, frying pan–style that the Russians have used in every tank since then. It is one of the best designs ever for deflecting enemy rounds, and it even eliminated shot traps. More important, its lean design meant no wasted space, which while minimizing any vestige of comfort for the crew, gave them superior protection, as the turret is guarded by 230 mm—11 inches—of steel armor plate. Put another way, the JS-III had as much as 70 mm more armor in the turret as the JS-II, yet still weighed *the same*, and was a foot shorter to boot! In all fairness, however, it was very unreliable; the JS-III was, after all, still a heavy tank!

JS-III (photo by author,
U.S. Army Ordnance Museum, Aberdeen Proving Ground)

JS-III (photo by author,
U.S. Army Ordnance Museum, Aberdeen Proving Ground)

JS-III (photo by author,
U.S. Army Ordnance Museum, Aberdeen Proving Ground)

None of these reached the front in time to fight the Germans, and the first public display came on September 7, 1945 at an Allied victory parade in Berlin, when fifty-two JS-IIIs took part. There are a number of ways to express the reaction of Western military representatives, most of them vulgar, but let us simply say that their jaws dropped. At that time the most advanced tank the Americans had was the spanking new, just introduced M26 Pershing; this had a 90 mm gun and 100 mm of armor. This disparity led to the subsequent development of heavy tanks like the U.S. M103 and the British Conqueror. More important, the threat of the JS-III influenced the design of some of the most successful Western tanks and equipment of the early Cold War era, tanks like the U.S. M48 Patton, the German Leopard I, the French AMX-30, and above all, the British L7 105 mm cannon, the best tank gun between the end of World War II and the recent introduction of the 120 mm generation of smooth-bore guns on tanks like the M1A1 Abrams. Even then, when the Israelis in M48s encountered Egyptians using JS-IIIs during the 1967 Six Days' War, they found their 90 mm guns could not penetrate their opponent's thick armor. Only superior training and maneuverability, plus a much faster rate of fire, saved the day, albeit with significant casualties. After this, the Israelis started thinking about new tanks of their own, leading to the development of the Merkava series, still one of the world's best tanks.

13

LIGHT TANKS

PLENTY OF NATIONS built and used light tanks in World War II, but generally speaking the results were disappointing. Most of this, in all fairness, stemmed from a lack of understanding of what light tanks could—and more important, could not—do on the battlefield. Usually, they were used as a form of cavalry, for reconnaissance and light screening, duties some of them could perform reasonably well.

On some subliminal level, however, a tank is still, no matter what, a tank, or in other words, a hard hitting, steel-armored, and cannon-wielding fighting vehicle, and often has to fight as such. When a light tank meets a heavier tank, however, the results are usually not all that positive for the slighter vehicle, and neither the Russians nor the Germans, the leading practitioners of tank warfare in World War II, were ever even close to being satisfied with the various models they used, and then discarded.

Instead, the one successful design was the American M24 Chaffee, clearly the best light tank of World War II (George Forty and Christopher Chant, two tank writers and experts, both emphasize this; in separate books, they felt compelled to add "without doubt," to the word "best").[5]

M24 Chaffee (photo by author,
U.S. Army Ordnance Museum, Aberdeen Proving Ground)

M24 CHAFFEE

By 1942, the results of the fighting in North Africa had indicated that America needed a new light tank, and the resulting process produced a winner. This time, designers eschewed the slab sides, the high profile, the cumbersome suspensions of so many American tanks, and created one of the most graceful tanks of the war. The M24 was relatively low at eight feet, one inch, and borrowed from the M18 Hellcat its torsion bar suspension, which was far superior to the suspensions on the various models of Shermans and M3 and M5 light tanks. Armor was relatively thin—this was a light tank, after all—with a maximum of 2.5 inches, but the glacis plate had a severe slope, and the M24's turret boasted the most fluid lines of any American armored vehicle of the war. With a pair of Cadillac V-8 engines, it could also spurt ahead at 35 mph on good roads. Both the engines and the Hydra-matic transmission were very reliable.

This little buggy also had something of a kick, better than the 37 mm of its predecessors, though still, of course, far below anything on a medium, let alone a heavy tank. It carried a light weight, low velocity, light recoil 75 mm gun that originally derived from the famous French 75 field piece, but had been drastically modified to be installed in the B-25 bomber. This had far less punch than the none-too-effective 75 mm in the Sherman, but did pack a useful HE round with considerable explosive heft.

Out in the field, the M24 proved a valuable asset, a good reconnaissance tank for the recon squadrons. On rare occasions, it actually got into fights with larger tanks and won, such as the time a few M24s accidently confronted a couple of Tigers outside Domagen. The American crews' fast instincts saved them, as the nimble Chaffees with their faster rotating turrets quickly maneuvered into position in the Tigers' rear and pumped out rounds that set off internal explosions within the German tanks.

But generally speaking, that was not an activity that anyone with a sane mind would engage in, given the choice, and the Chaffee was better off sticking to support for the infantry in their half-tracks. The M24's 75 mm high explosive round was a big step up from the one launched from the 37 mm cannon on the earlier M3 and M5 light tanks; thus, it was capable of inflicting much more damage on the kinds of strongpoints the Germans had thrown up in towns and cities, making it an effective weapon for armor-infantry cooperation.

The M24 soldiered on after the war, giving good service in Korea, where it tried to stem the tide of the first North Korean attacks, but could not stand up against armies equipped with T-34/85s. By then, of course, the initial era of light tanks was drawing to a close; even by the end of World War II most American tankers would have preferred that the Chaffees be replaced by an equivalent number of Shermans. After that conflict, few new light tanks were introduced during the long years of the Cold War, although the concept is being revived in the twenty-first century because of the demand for armor that can be quickly and readily airlifted into a combat zone.

Up to this point I have covered the major strands of analysis on tanks, but it is time to diverge a tad and have some fun. Given that tanks are considered the decisive land weapon of World War II, I thought it might be either informative or amusing, or both, to pursue some other discussions on issues that range from being somewhat important to the bizarre and even frivolous. I call these my "sidebar" topics, in that they are of some interest, but take place outside the main line of argument.

14

THE SHERMAN TANK: WAS IT REALLY THAT GOOD OR THAT BAD?

THE M4 SHERMAN, of course, was the dominant tank of the Western Allies, produced in such record numbers that it equipped not only the American forces, but those of all the other Western Allies as well, including the large British forces and the Free French and Polish units; several thousand were also sent to the Soviet Union to help on the Eastern Front.

For almost sixty years now, debate has raged over the Sherman. Some historians, experts, and former users argue that it comes close to being the best tank of the war: well-balanced, reliable, easy to produce, it was a prototype of the Main Battle Tank, second only to the T-34 in that regard.

Others go in the exact opposite direction, citing the Sherman's abject failure in the latter part of the war, the pronounced ability of Panthers and Tigers to destroy it at exaggerated ranges, and the fact that they seemed almost invulnerable to the Sherman's best shots. Again, we hear the learned voices, and those of men who fought and saw many of their friends die in these machines. For

U.S. M4 Sherman tank (photo by author,
U.S. Army Ordnance Museum, Aberdeen Proving Ground)

these individuals, the Sherman is best summed up in the title of a
book by Belton Cooper, an armored officer who served throughout
Europe: *Death Traps*.

While there is a lot of discussion, analysis, argument, and con-
tention about tanks, no other piece of World War II armor conjures
up anywhere near this vast a disagreement. So which is true: was
the Sherman really up to the job, or was it such a dismal failure?

To make sense of this argument, I am setting up my discussion in three parts: first, what was good about the M4. Next, what
was bad. Finally, I will provide analysis, pull it all together, and
deliver my verdict from on high.

SHERMAN: THE POSITIVES

There is absolutely no question in my mind that any objective
look at the Sherman reveals a number of sterling features, some
of them, in fact, the most advanced of any tank of the war.

The greatest attribute of the Sherman was its reliability, something the Germans marveled at. This is often misunderstood, as

most people are so impressed with tanks—massive steel machines that seem indestructible—that what is frequently overlooked is how fragile they are, and how prone to breakdown.

Yes, these are weapons designed to do some pretty incredible things: go over all kinds of obstacles, for example, and various forms of terrain, better than any wheeled vehicle known. And they can withstand a large wedge of metal traveling at speeds that make a jet fighter look like granny's Model T, slamming head on into them.

Despite this, there are a number of things that can cause a tank to stop in its tracks. No suspension, for example, ever devised can really handle endless amounts of rough ground, which is why tanks always tried to stay on roads or flat ground whenever possible. Think about the Battle of the Bulge: the key position was Bastogne, a crossroads town. The fact that the Germans fought so hard to get in, and the Americans so desperately to keep them out, indicates just how important a hub of good roads was to a World War II armored force.

This is true, by the way, for their modern-day counterparts as well. Even the M1 Abrams, the best tank in the world today according to many experts, can snap its torsion bars far easier than is normally realized.

The worst problem a tank faces, however, is heat. Take a look at your car and notice just how many devices it has to disperse the heat of the engine and other systems: the fan, the cooling system, the front vent that ensures a smooth flow of air throughout the vehicle. If these were not in place, or if they fail, heat will knock an engine out faster than any factor short of a shaped-charge warhead.

Now think about a tank. It is a sealed box, with the fewer openings the better; designers of most post–World War II tanks, for example, removed the bow machine gun so that the front plate would be a solid sheet of metal with nothing to weaken it. If designers could figure out how to do it, tanks would be made up of welded steel with nothing to disrupt the integrity of the armor.

So then what do you do with the heat? All tanks have places

where the heat is dispersed—vents or fans—but the designer always walks a fine line, trying to provide the maximum cooling from the minimum openings. When his measurements are wrong, or when the tank's engine is stressed beyond what anyone planned for, the vehicle overheats and is out of action. It is a tricky matter indeed.

So reliability is not a factor tankers take for granted. And on this scale the Sherman was superb. American crews would land in France in the summer of 1944 and—if they beat the odds and survived—make it through to the end of the war, in the same vehicle, without a single major breakdown. One British tanker reported how his Sherman took the crew through and out of the bocage, to the fight for the River Seine and then the battle for Le Havre. Next it went by tank transporter to Holland where it helped defend the Nijmegen-Eindhoven corridor during Market Garden, followed by plunging into the Ardennes during the Battle of the Bulge. There was only one mechanical problem throughout all of this, when the rubber came off a couple of bogie wheels, a remarkable record. American treads also lasted longer, by the way; about 2,500 miles, compared to 500 miles for their German counterparts. Some authorities claim that the Sherman's reliability far exceeded even that of the T-34. George Patton observed, "In mechanical endurance and ease of maintenance our tanks are infinitely superior to any other," and he was right.[6]

Reliability kept American tanks in the field at a higher rate than the Germans managed, but massive production reinforced this ability to always have large numbers of Shermans available for any Allied attack. In 1939, the U.S. Army had a smaller tank force than Poland, and in 1940 only 330 new tanks were built. But this rose to 24,997 in 1942 (more than the total of German tank production for the entire war), and then went up to 29,487 the year after. By the end of the war, the United States had built roughly 287,000 armored vehicles of all kinds, more than any other nation.

In many ways the hero of this part of the story is not a tanker at all, but a businessman named Walter Knudsen. Knudsen was president of General Motors and a member of the National Defense Advisory Committee set up in 1940 to plan war production.

At that time there was only one kind of factory that could produce a tank. Think about it: what kind of plant deals with large vehicles made up of heavy pieces of steel? Locomotive factories, of course, and that was exactly where tanks got made in Russia and Germany, in converted facilities originally geared up to produce those big engines that haul the trains.

Knudsen argued against this. Locomotive plants were used to filling small "bespoke" orders for one piece at a time, and could not handle the flood of weapons America would require. The only industry that had the expertise to handle this would be one familiar with mass-production methods, and that meant the auto makers. While the idea was self-serving, it also revolutionized wartime production, not only in the United States, but around the world.

Knudsen then called K. T. Keller, president of the Chrysler Corporation, and asked if he could set up a new tank arsenal on behalf of the government. Keller sent a team of engineers out to Rock Island Arsenal to look things over, and they came back with a lot of ideas and a full set of drawings for the latest tanks, to the tune of 186 pounds of blueprints. On June 17, the engineers started working on a plan, which had to cover minor issues like the size of the building, its equipment, the nature of the workforce, and everything else needed to turn out tanks from scratch. Unbelievably, they finished a month later, and Chrysler presented the Department of War with a proposal on July 17. Construction began, just outside Detroit, in September 1940 on a 113 acre site, and was completed by March 1941. A year later, it had built 2,000 medium tanks. Later on, as the need for tanks continued to grow, the Chrysler Detroit Tank Arsenal would be joined by facilities run by Ford and by the Fisher Body Works of General Motors, and even firms like American Locomotive Company (2,300 Shermans), the Baldwin Locomotive Works (1,245 Shermans), and the Lima Locomotive Works

(1,655 Shermans) helped set records. By the time they were all done, 49,234 Shermans of all models had come off the lines.

Another production factor also played a critical part in the Sherman story. American leaders knew that they would have to do something no other country had to: move a gigantic army across thousands of miles of oceans. To this end they created the Liberty Ship, which could be built faster, and in larger numbers, than any other ship before or since, mass production of the seas if you will. And one wonderful thing about the Sherman's measurements was that it fit beautifully and snugly into the holds of these Liberty Ships, so that the maximum number of tanks could be carried on each trip, thus making possible the Allied invasion of Europe.

There were some other great features of the Sherman tank as well as its availability, factors that made a crucial difference in combat. The Sherman, for example, had the best turret traversing system of any tank in the war, substantially better than anything in any German tank, and especially better than those in the Tiger and even the Panther. Where these were cumbersome, jerky, and slow, the Sherman's was easy to use, extremely fast, and quite nimble and sensitive to the touch. A Sherman crew, for example, could move their turret through a full 360 degree revolution in less than ten seconds; this is fast enough to make you dizzy, but it also indicates just how little time was spent in a small movement, the kind that happens when you suddenly see an enemy tank off to the side. A 90 degree turn, for example, only took two to three seconds. And if anybody doubts how good that was, the Tiger took, depending on what system was used, a bare minimum of twenty-five seconds to turn the turret in a full circle, and at worst this could take a full minute. What all this meant was crucial in combat: the Sherman could get off not only the first shot, but also a few of them (some experts say as many as four or five) before the Tiger could do a thing.

It also meant the Sherman could maneuver around and then move the turret accordingly, a tactic helped enormously by the fact that the Sherman had the first and only gyro-stabilized weapon in the war. Primitive by modern standards, it kept the gun steady in terms of elevation only, using a hydraulic system. While the system was so complicated that many crews often entered battle without turning it on, when they did use the new gizmo, it meant that the Sherman was the only tank on the battlefield that could move over any hillock, any depression, and the gun would stay fixed on the target, in terms of height, at least.

Oh, and while we're at it, the Sherman also carried an FM radio. This gave a far clearer sound than the AM radios used exclusively in German tanks, and beat hell out of what the Russians had, which was nothing for the first part of the war.

Finally, a couple of other points in defense of the Sherman. Its optics, while nowhere near as good as those of German tanks, were superior to the equipment in the T-34. If the gasoline engine it used increased the proclivity to catch fire, this was based on the reasonably rational decision that since the United States had already standardized on gasoline for all support vehicles, and since fuel would be hauled enormous distances, it made sense to use only one type and not introduce a second—diesel—into a system that was already way too complicated.

Another issue that it is only fair to discuss when defending the Sherman, in this case concerning vulnerability, is that by the time it saw heavy action in France and Germany, the U.S. was constantly on the attack. This almost always leads to heavier casualties than for the defenders, since you have to stick your nose out and advance on the enemy.

There is no question, therefore, that the Sherman was a handy vehicle and an initial attempt, along with the T-34 series, to create a universal tank, a rather refreshing thought after looking at the Germans' constant tinkering. When combined with innovative American ground tactics, it could do a job, and there are accounts from panzer commanders that they respected these opponents and did not consider them weak at all.

SHERMAN: THE NEGATIVES

Then why is the Sherman dissed by so many, spoken of with such contempt and derogation? The fact was, the Sherman had terrible shortcomings, ones the Germans ruthlessly exploited as soon as the Western allies landed in France and began slugging it out directly with the Wehrmacht.

Let's do this by the numbers, starting with that all-important discussion of firepower. If this doesn't work, you can't kill anything, and you get knocked out instead.

Most M4 Shermans carried a 75 mm gun that had a very good high explosive round; in fact, this dual capability was one of the best features of the gun, ahead of what the British were doing at the time, on a par with what the Russians and Germans were developing. But unfortunately, it also used an armor piercing round traveling at only 2,030 fps that could penetrate a mere 62 mm of armor at 1,000 meters. This compares unfavorably even to the L/48 on the last versions of the Panzer Mk IV (2,461 fps), but is just pathetic once you bring in the second generation of World War II tanks: the T-34/85's regular armor piercing round could go through 102 mm at 1,000 meters, and its tungsten-cored round was devastating at short range, able to penetrate 138 mm at 500 meters. The Tiger I with its 88 mm L/56 could do in 102 mm of armor sloped at 30 degrees at 1,000 meters, and forget about the Panther. Its long 75 mm cannon fired an armor piercing round at 3,300 fps, which could slam through 111 mm of steel at a full 1,000 meters.

Even when the Sherman tried to improve, it still could not play in these leagues. By 1944 a number of tanks—and soon all—were being upgunned to a longer barreled gun (L/53) that could take a larger length cartridge with the same diameter (i.e., the same shell but with more powder), designated 76 mm to differentiate it from its predecessor. This brought velocity up to 2,600 fps and increased penetration at 1,000 meters to 89 mm, which was still not that good when compared to what the Panther could do. One way to understand this is to note that the armor piercing projectile of the Sherman's 76 mm and the Panther's 75 mm actually weighed about the same, but the cartridge case—the part filled with powder to send the shell on its way—on the Panther's round was longer and wider than that used for even the Americans' 90 mm round, the most powerful U.S. weapon of this sort fielded during the war. When the Shermans got a limited distribution APCR (Armor Piercing Composite Rigid) round capable of 3,400 fps, it still bounced off a Tiger's armor at longer ranges. And the 76 mm high explosive round was even inferior to the older 75 mm round in one crucial capacity: because it needed thicker walls to handle the greater velocity, it carried less than half the explosive filler of its predecessor, making it far less effective as a weapon against fortifications or infantry.

In fact, the only time the Sherman ever managed to carry an adequate gun was when it mounted the British 17 pounder anti-tank cannon (more on this when we compare it to the 88 mm),

Late-model Sherman tank (M4A3E8) with long-barreled 75 mm gun
(photo by author, American Society of Military History Military Museum, South El Monte, CA)

but even here the Americans denied that this could be put into a Sherman turret, and it took the British to design a mounting that worked just fine, thank you. Because of limited British production capacity compared with the United States, however, relatively few of these machines—called the Sherman Firefly—made it into the field.

The result of this situation was that the Sherman could not accomplish the primary mission that tanks were supposed to do by that point in their development, kill enemy tanks. One Sherman gunner told how he and his unit came across a line of German tanks moving across an open field, perfect targets. The American guns, he reported, "all opened fire on them, but we had just about as well have fired our shots straight up in the air for all the good we could do. Every round would bounce off and wouldn't do a bit of damage. I fired at one 800 yds away, he had his side to me. I hit him from the lap of the turret to the bottom and from the front of the tank to the back . . . but he never halted. . . . [I]f we had a gun with plenty of muzzle velocity we would have wiped them out." Ominously, he added, "I have found it is silly to try to fight the German tank."[7]

Other Sherman operators told similar tales. Corporal Frances Vierling saw "twenty-five or even more of our rounds fired and ricochet off the enemy attackers," while Sergeant Harold Fulton found that when he attacked a Tiger it was even worse, "Every time one of the APs hit the tank you could see them ricochet two and three hundred feet into the air." The most dismal story of all comes from Nat Frankel, whose memoirs of his service as a tanker with Patton's Third Army included an almost comical tale. Frankel described how "a monster of a Tiger 6 [i.e., Panzer Mk VI or Tiger I] was pivoting not thirty yards in front of me. I fired three shots at it, figuring to force it backward. All three shots bounced off the side and ricocheted harmlessly." Then, the kicker, "What do I see but a German officer stick his head out of the turret and smile at me! He then proceeded to pull a white handkerchief out of his pocket and wipe it against the side of his machine, where my bullets had skidded. He smiled again as if to forgive me for scratching his property; then he replaced his handkerchief in his pocket."[8]

This enormous shortcoming combined with inadequate armor and design, created a perilous situation. The front plate of the Sherman sloped at either 60 or 47 degrees (depending on which model hull is being discussed), but was a bare 50 mm thick (2 inches), and the turret front only reached 88 mm (3.5 inches); even the British Matilda II, which began limited production in 1938, had better frontal armor than that. The side plates, meanwhile, had no slope at all, and were entirely vertical. At the same time, the Sherman was also the tallest tank on the battlefield, making it an above-average target; its straight, slabsided profile stretched to over nine feet (eleven feet on later models), which was about the same height as the much heavier and more formidable Tigers and Panthers.[9]

This meant, simply put, that the Sherman was frightfully easy to penetrate and destroy, frightfully easy to have its crew members killed and maimed. There are stories of the Tiger's armor-piercing rounds entering the front of a Sherman and going out the rear, with nothing anywhere to impede their progress. Even worse, there are cases of Tigers and Panthers knocking out a Sherman even though they were firing through a brick wall, and most tragic of all, where they took out a Sherman by firing *through another Sherman* to get the shot; two American crews were destroyed with one German round. Gil McNeese, a sergeant with the First Special Service Force, claimed, "The Tigers were knocking off those Shermans as if they weren't there. I remember seeing a Sherman tank run in behind a small building, trying to get away from this fire. A Tiger punched an 88 right through the building and right through the turret of the Sherman. They didn't have a chance." One German told interviewers, "Our gunners see your tanks coming . . . and they say to each other, 'Here comes another Ronson.' Why do the Americans do this for us? Bang! and it burns like twenty haystacks. All the people [inside], my God. . . . Those funny little tanks with the little guns and so high and straight we can see them from a long way in our gunsights. Those square sides, and thin, the armor." Finally he asked, "Why does the country of Detroit send their men out to die in these things?"[10]

The problem with armor, combined with the lack of firepower, created an extreme situation for American tankers: because German tanks were both better armed and armored, they could kill Shermans at long ranges, whereas Shermans had to get very close or else maneuver in so they could hit at the sides or rear. Either way, it put Allied drivers in dire jeopardy for a long while until they could get in adequate range or position, during which time the larger German tanks were virtually invulnerable. The 75 mm gunned Sherman could not penetrate the front armor of a Panther even if it put the muzzle of its cannon right up to the front plate and fired, but the Panther could destroy a Sherman from the front at over 1,500 meters. If the Sherman could score a hit on the Panther's weaker side plates at a few hundred meters, the Panther could do the same to a Sherman at 3,000 to 4,000 meters.

And while we're at it, the Sherman had a number of other shortcomings as well, pretty serious ones. Instead of a diesel it used a gasoline engine that had a fairly strong tendency to catch fire, even under the best of conditions; modern day collectors often have someone standing by with a fire extinguisher whenever they start one up. During wartime this meant that when struck, they would explode; Frankel told how it was: "But when that gas got hit, your options were, to say the least, limited. Oh, we had a fire extinguisher, but that was for overheated engines; it was useless for an exploded tank." He then described the proper procedure, and its folly: "Now, there are two ways to get out. One was via the turret; the other was via a trapdoor on the opposite side of the driver from the bow gun. Often the turret would be inaccessible . . . if the machine was hit badly, particularly if it was knocked on its side, the trapdoor would jam as well. At best you have ninety seconds to get out that door; if it jammed, you would need fifty of those seconds to push it open. That would leave forty seconds for three men to squeeze out. Tick, tick, tick, boom!"[11]

In addition, the one thing that it was supposed to excel in, mobility, it didn't. While admittedly the Sherman was fast, it was not all that sure-footed, as its thin tracks gave it a fairly high ground pressure, and it could sink in mud where a Panther or a T-34 could keep going. Even worse, tanks like the Tiger had gears that enabled it to spin around while stationary, which meant they could turn practically within their own length. The Sherman, on the other hand, had no such mechanicals, and its minimum turning circle was around sixty feet. In tight places, such as fights on thin roads or in narrow streets, where the ability to shift and turn was critical, this became a major shortcoming. One American sergeant asked, "How can we outflank them when all they have to do is pivot and keep their frontal armor toward us?" then added, "We've got a good tank—for parades and training purposes—but for combat they are just potential coffins."[12]

That last remark highlighted the real consequence of the Sherman design, one that was paid for in blood. The Third Armored Division landed in Normandy with a complement of 232 M4 Sherman tanks. By the time Germany surrendered, the division had had 648 Shermans totally destroyed, while another 700 had been knocked out, repaired, and returned to battle. A loss rate, in other words, of *580 percent* in eleven months. In only two days, the Second Armored Division lost 57 tanks and took 363 casualties. In the Fourth Armored Division there was standing policy that troops could only help crews from destroyed tanks who had left their vehicles, and they were forbidden from removing bodies, for fear that what they saw after a German shell hit would be too demoralizing. After the Battle of the Bulge it got so bad in some units that they could not field full crews, and tanks went out with, instead of the normal five-man complement, four or even three troopers, the bare minimum required to run a tank, but all that was available after heavy casualties. A tank commander commented with disgust,

"Lack of a principal gun with sufficient penetrating ability to knock out the German opponent has cost us more tanks and skilled men to man more tanks than the failure of our crews, not to mention the heartbreak and sense of defeat I and other men have felt. To see twenty-five or even many more of our rounds fired and ricochet off the enemy attackers. To be finally hit, *once*, and we climb from a burning, blackened, and now a useless pile of scrap iron. It would have yet been a tank had it mounted a gun."[13]

What makes this so tragic, and what incites such anger, is that some American officials knew about the shortcomings, and others should have. *Life*, for example, carried a story in its March 26, 1945, issue called "The Battle of the Tanks" that made clear the Sherman's failures, comparing it disastrously to the JS-II and the Tiger II. Almost simultaneously, the *New York Times* ran a series of articles between March 18 and March 20, 1945 that excoriated the Sherman. It claimed that the introduction of the heavier M26 Pershing was "prima facie evidence, despite prior misleading statements from some of our generals, that the Sherman is not equal to the German . . . models" and that it proved the claims of American tankers that they needed a better tank, pleas that had produced no results for a period of two years or more. Even Ike was out in the cold; in a famous passage from Omar Bradley's memoirs, the Supreme Commander reacted with anger when he found out that the advanced version of the Sherman's main gun still wouldn't do the job, "You mean our 76 won't knock the Panthers out? I thought it was going to be the wonder gun of the war. . . . Why is it that I am always the last to know about this stuff? Ordnance told me the 76 would take care of anything the Germans had. Now I find out you can't knock out a damn thing with it."[14]

Even worse, however, were the comments by soldiers to the *Times*. Sergeant Ernest Holland exclaimed, "we're just out-tanked and outgunned, that's all. We don't mind the lack of armor on our tanks as much as the lack of firepower . . ."; and Sergeant John Gorzalski commented, "you can't go against a Tiger with a peashooter." Sergeant Raymond Kasner showed the gap between the equipment and the men, on the other hand, when he explained, "Our tank guns just won't penetrate the . . . Tiger or the Panther from the front. It's lucky we have so many tanks. That's the only way we can outmaneuver and outflank them," but then added, "If they'd give me a Mk V (Panther) I'd take on any of the bastards."[15]

The most powerful comments of all came from an unidentified second lieutenant in the cavalry, recovering from wounds. "Since I have spent three years in a tank platoon," he observed, "doing everything, and at one time or another have held every position, and have read everything on armor I could get my hands on . . . I would like to get this off my chest. No statement, claim or promise made by any part of the Army," he argued, "can justify thousands of dead and wounded tankmen, or thousands of others who depended on the tank for support. . . . Whoever was responsible for supplying the Army with tanks is guilty of supplying material inferior to its enemy counterpart for at least two years or more. How anyone can escape punishment for neglecting such a vital weapon of war is beyond me."[16]

Belton Cooper, in the preface to his book *Death Traps*, wrote that the disadvantages of the M4 Sherman "not only resulted in tremendous pain and suffering and losses in personnel and armor, but also delayed the successful conclusion of the war in Europe." How, indeed, could such a thing have occurred?[17]

There are a number of reasons the story of the Sherman worked out the way it did, some of which we have mentioned before. The United States, for example, stressed high production runs and like the Soviet Union, was loathe to break this up to introduce new models, depending on sheer numbers to overcome all obstacles. In addition, there was the problem with transit; American officials had to weigh just how many fewer tanks would go overseas if new, heavier models were introduced, and whether or not this was a worthwhile tradeoff.

These reasons at least make some kind of sense, but there were other powerful factors at work here, some of them neither as smart nor as noble.

SHERMAN: THE UGLY

The Sherman was plagued, for example, by the pettiest of jurisdictional disputes. Three separate departments within the U.S. Army all vied for control of this project and engaged in some of the worst bickering of the war. When it came to deciding what the Sherman would look like and what should go into it, Army Ground Forces (AGF) had a powerful say, but so did the Armored Board, and you could not keep out the Ordnance Board either.

The result was endless wrangling over small issues, and a compromise to permit a number of favored—and erroneous—assumptions. The AGF, which created and fought for the tank destroyer doctrine (see below) wanted a light, fast, exploitation tank; the Armored Board became fixated on the Sherman as its exclusive war winner; and the Ordnance Board provided bad information on the effectiveness of the 75 mm and 76 mm guns and had to champion them in order to not look bad. Throughout the war, Ordnance never tested its guns against anything but vertical armor plate and never took into account the relative quality of German steel versus the quality of the American product, nor of improvements in metallurgy that went on during the war. Its conflict, however, with other powerful factions meant that the bureaucratic forces to keep the Sherman as it was were strong, and those in favor of switching to a better tank were weak.

The Sherman's development was also hobbled, however, by flawed doctrine. Because America did not enter the war until after the initial German victories, it had a relatively free period to consider blitzkrieg and devise tactics to beat it. Like everyone else, the top ranks of the U.S. Army faced this vision of massed tanks, tanks everywhere, descending on their own hopeless forces. Whereas the Russians realized immediately what is now the

acknowledged wisdom—that it takes a tank to kill another tank—
the Americans decided to *not* use their tank forces for that mission. Instead AGF, led by Lieutenant General Lesley McNair, the
leading advocate of this idea, came up with the notion that a force
of tank destroyers should be built and organized into separate units
to deal exclusively with this kind of threat.

Thus, the official U.S. doctrine throughout World War II went
something like this: when German panzer units attacked and
threatened a breakthrough, tanks should not be used to fight them.
Instead, we would develop vast fleets of tank destroyers, which
would be light, extremely fast vehicles with thinner armor but the
heaviest guns possible, that would rush to the endangered sector
and neutralize the threat. Only after that had happened, the tanks
would then move out in the exploitation role, traveling quickly
over the countryside and produce fast, stunning victories.[18]

An interesting idea, this, but also one that had little to do with
reality. Any plan that involves a type of weapon not having to fight
another type of weapon usually founders when that is exactly the
kind of combat that occurs in the real world. Tanks fought tanks,
and tank destroyers, in less and less demand as the panzer forces
got worn down, but with more powerful guns, wound up being
used as field artillery by commanders who needed support and
were not about to let these weapons sit by idly.

But this doctrine had a lot of ramifications, none of them good.
Tank destroyers were in a separate command from the tank units,
for example, and had their own training and doctrine. This just
made an already complicated Table of Organization even worse.

But the biggest consequence was how it affected tank design.
Because of this concept, the Sherman was always supposed to be
undergunned, in opposition to the tank destroyers. Remember the
upgraded 76 mm gun that did not appear on Shermans until later
in the war? By 1943 an earlier version had been mounted on the
M10 tank destroyer. The Sherman, instead, was reliable, light
(read: lightly armored), fast and nimble, perfect for breakout, which

it really did excel in during the gorgeous summer and early fall months of 1944 when the U.S. Army poured across France.

No one ever successfully challenged this doctrine, in part because of General McNair's fervent belief in it, but also because of both his clout and his intransigency. After North Africa, when reports started to come in that tank destroyers were not such a good idea, McNair wrote that he remained "confident that the track we are on—in . . . tank destroyers—is both sound and not in jeopardy" that "developments in Africa only serve to demonstrate the soundness of this conception." Later, when comments from Europe as late as November 1943—this is after we had faced Tigers in Italy—urged him to start work on a 90 mm armed tank, McNair replied, "I see no reason to alter our previous stand . . . essentially that we should defeat Germany by use of the M-4 series of medium tanks. There has been no factual developments overseas, so far as I know to challenge the superiority of the M-4. An increase in armor or gun power can have no purpose other than to engage in tank vs. tank action—which is unsound. Moreover, such a tank would be disadvantageous in carrying out the primary mission of armor—to defeat those elements of the enemy which are vulnerable to tanks." He then reiterated, "The answer to heavy tanks is the tank destroyer."[19]

McNair's ability to hold to these positions for so long only points toward the largest factor of all in explaining the Sherman's shortcomings. Bluntly put, the most important reason for the Sherman's failures is that the United States entered the primary arena of the European theater relatively late, that the Second Front did not start until the last eleven months of the war. Up until then, the U.S. was fighting in secondary theaters, facing relatively small pieces of the German army; we never did, never had to participate in an arms race in tanks, as the Russians and Germans did. That race, instead, was based not on theory, but on the reality of combat, which is merciless in exposing flaws in both technology and tactics. Within months of confronting the main body of the Wehrmacht, Americans knew they needed something better.

Permit me to expand on this argument. War is a relentless evaluator, in that it exposes any defect in the harshest way. From the time Germany launched Barbarossa, the majority of German forces were on the Eastern Front, a situation that would never change throughout the war, although the relative proportions would.

This meant that from 1942 on, after the initial shock of Mk III and IV against T-34, the Germans and the Russians were engaged in—locked in would be a better term—an arms race in tanks, one that produced, as war does, the best equipment of the conflict; as Charles Baily put it, "The inadequacies of German and Russian equipment were quickly revealed by large, frequent tank battles."[20]

Thus, the problems with American armor in World War II were not because the nation designed and fielded a bad machine, but because it never moved past its initial steps since it didn't have to. In early to mid-1942, the Sherman was one of the three top tanks in the world, and a good argument can be made that it was the best of them all. It had comparable armor and a better gun than either the Panzer Mk III or the early Mk IV. The T-34 had better armor and a harder-hitting gun, but featured terrible internal conditions that vastly diminished its combat capabilities, such as the three-man crew and lack of a radio, and may have been less reliable. After the Battle of El Alamein, General Erwin Rommel wrote, "Their new tank, the General Sherman . . . showed itself superior to any of ours."[21]

That moment in the sun, however, lasted for only a few months, as the Germans and the Russians, fused in arch-enemy conflict, moved on in a hurry, while America, basking in its relative lack of combat activity, stood still, rather than implementing the heavier tank that would become the M26 Pershing.

This, therefore, becomes the crucial factor, because it permitted the other ones. When one reads about the squabbles, the natural question that arises is whether or not such disputes would have been permitted if U.S. forces were totally engaged in fighting the Germans. The answer is obvious, backed up by the real-time evidence that, in fact, changes did occur rather quickly once we finally landed in Europe and started punching it out with the German panzer divisions. Compare this, furthermore, to what happened in aircraft design; by 1942 to 1943 both in Europe and the Pacific, American planes were fighting all-out, in large numbers, against the best the enemy had to throw back at us. Improvements came fast and furious, ever newer and better models, in contrast to the Sherman, which relatively stood still for too long; as the old saying goes, more technological change occurs in a year of war than in a decade of peace. Mark Hayward, an expert on the British Firefly version of this tank, wrote that the "Sherman in 1944 was virtually obsolete."[22]

The best line I have ever read on the Sherman in Western Europe came from Corporal Thomas McIane, who fought in M4s across France and Germany. He said that the Panther was superior to his tanks in both armor and armament, and then observed, "Our successes in Europe are a result of superiority in numbers and superiority in good cold guts, not a result of superior tanks."[23]

15

WHAT WAS THE BEST TANK DESTROYER?

HAVING BROUGHT UP THE TERM "tank destroyer" in the previous section, I thought it appropriate to turn to this form of armored vehicle next. After all, tank destroyers got built in record numbers; aside from tanks themselves, destroyers remain the most numerous armored fighting vehicles with full-powered armament built during the years of war.

There were two separate doctrines for tank destroyers (TDs) in World War II, two separate visions of how they should be used; this, in turn, determined what kind of weapons got designed. The American doctrine was just described, so let's start there.

Using this doctrine, the ideal American tank destroyer favored mobility over any other asset. Thus, the most prized version of TD the Americans ever built was not the M36, which carried a formidable 90 mm cannon, but the smaller, faster M18 Hellcat.

M18 HELLCAT

First fielded in 1944, the M18 squeezed a version of the 76 mm later installed in the Sherman into a relatively tiny turret (the gun had to

M18 Hellcat (Robert Bruce Military Photo Features)

be tilted at 45 degrees in order to make it fit), along with forty-five rounds of ammunition and three crew members. Armor was perilously thin at only 25 mm on the turret front and an astounding 13 mm on the glacis; this was the same as on the Panzer Mk I, which was considered inadequate even before the war started.

What made the Hellcat stand out from the crowd, however, was its unbelievable mobility. Using the torsion bar suspension later installed in the M24 Chaffee and any of a variety of engines that gave from 340 to 400 hp, the Hellcat became a speedy little bugger indeed.

How fast? By means of comparison, fast tanks in World War II went at 30 mph, and at 35 you were really moving. The Hellcat, on the other hand, is usually listed at 55 mph, a figure that was not matched until the M1 Abrams achieved this in the 1980s, thirty-five years or so later. In truth, the manual lists a mere 45 mph as cruising speed, but warns about loss of control once one goes 60 mph, implying that the vehicle could achieve that speed, and even higher; one test on experimental tracks showed that it could go over 75 mph, which is really astonishing. That meant, in other words, that the Hellcat could have beat the speed limit on a modern U.S. highway, and indeed, drivers remarked that handling this vehicle was like an outing with a sports car. If that vision of a Hellcat trying to pass on the left seems intimidating today, think of what its standard 55 mph must have looked like as this armored fighting machine zipped by motorists restricted to 35 mph because of wartime regulations!

Some accounts claim that tankers loved the Hellcat, but I am not so sure. It must have been a hell of a lot of fun to drive, and provided incredible mobility to sneak up on German armor. But when you did get into position, you had a somewhat outdated gun with which to do battle, one that still could not pierce frontal armor except at the closest of ranges. Also on the downside, the armor was ridiculously thin, and you cannot outrun a tank shell, no matter how fast you are. Keep in mind, too, the American tank destroyers were supposed to shuttle across the countryside to wherever the enemy had achieved penetration and knock them back. The tactics had to involve flitting across the landscape, firing and moving; but if an M18 got caught in a toe-to-toe conflict, it would crumble like a paper sack hit by an ice ball, the thin armor no match for even the smallest imaginable main gun. As we have said, it was not the most enlightened of concepts.

Add to this, however, one other piece of folly. Americans had a predilection, for some reason I have never been able to fathom, for open topped turrets. Yes, this had the advantages of lessening weight and providing superior observation, but the downsides were doozies. First of all, an open turret means that the crew is viciously vulnerable to any shellburst, any tree burst that goes off anywhere near it. Even worse, any soldier with a grenade can take it out with an easy toss; if you remember that the M18 had a terribly cramped turret (I have been in one), you start to get an idea of the kind of horror we are talking about. And finally, it exposes the crew to all the elements of the weather, which is downright mean-spirited, if you ask me. Nevertheless, every tank destroyer the U.S. made, plus its armored cars, had this nasty little feature.

Sometimes you see writers talking about the Hellcat as the best tank destroyer of the war, but they are, to be polite, overly enamored with American technology, or speed, or something. To really see what tank destroyers were like, and what they could do, we have to turn to the arena where the armored arms race took place, the Eastern Front.

Both the Germans and the Russians envisioned tank destroyer tactics in similar ways; both saw these weapons as ones that worked from the sidelines, positioning themselves on the flanks and picking off enemy tanks with powerful anti-tank guns. They were not supposed to be all that mobile, and none of these weapons had a turret, all of them carrying their large cannon in some form of ball mounting. The Germans, as usual, expected their tank destroyers to work in large groupings that would employ considerable collective firepower. The commander of the unit would carefully study the terrain, choose the best ambush positions possible, and then lay in wait and decimate an enemy column. When used in the attack, they would be employed the same way the Russians used theirs, to stay back a little or on the sides and provide direct fire support against enemy armor, as well as protecting against flank attacks. Russian tank destroyer units also worked with the slower, heavy tank units, as their considerably faster speed enabled them to move quickly across the battlefield to protect the advancing behemoths.

This doctrine clearly was more modest and made a lot more sense than what the Americans believed in, and it also produced the best tank destroyers of the war.

JAGDTIGER

One weapon that does not measure up, however, is what is, unfortunately, the best known tank destroyer of them all, the Jagdtiger, or "Hunting Tiger"; fame and quality do not necessarily go together. Yes, it is true that the Jagdtiger was the biggest armored

Jagdtiger (photo by author,
U.S. Army Ordnance Museum, Aberdeen Proving Ground)

vehicle ever fielded during the war. Based on the Tiger II chassis, the frontal armor was hardly sloped at all, but that really did not matter much, as it was 250 mm (10 inches) thick. I have rapped on the front of a Jagdtiger with my knuckles, and while that action produces a tinny, metallic sound on most armored vehicles, when you do it to this one, you feel like you are tapping on a mountainside, with infinite depth. One writer said this armor was "impenetrable by anything short of a battleship."[24]

The Jagdtiger weighed a titanic seventy-five tons, and a big tank destroyer needs a big gun. It got one, a 128 mm L/55 cannon that weighed 7,380 pounds all by itself, more than some early tanks. This was the largest gun ever mounted on an armored, tracked vehicle during the war, and, by comparison, the standard NATO tank gun in the twenty-first century is 120 mm, albeit a far more powerful weapon than the one on the Jadgtiger.

That 128 mm gun was still a mighty impressive weapon. It fired a 62-pound armor-piercing shell that could penetrate 230 mm

(9.1 inches) of armor at 1,000 meters, and far more worrisome, 173 mm at 3,000 meters, a distance at which most tank guns lost both punch and accuracy. George Forty described how in the summer of 1948 he came across "what seemed to have been an entire regiment of Sherman tanks which had been completely annihilated. There were Shermans lying on heaps everywhere one looked, turrets blown off, hulls ripped apart." The Shermans had been attacked from the flank, and when they and their follow-up units had turned to face the enemy, a lack of covering terrain meant they remained easy targets. Even years later, their tormentor still sat on the top of an overlooking hill, a single, by now burned out Jadgtiger.[25]

So why wasn't this the best tank destroyer of World War II? You can probably figure out the answers by now. Despite the enormous weight, the Germans kept using engines designed for smaller vehicles, the same engine as in the Tiger I and the King Tiger. This gave it speeds as low as 9 mph cross country, which meant this was not an attacking vehicle at all, but a fast moving pillbox. That kind of strain also took its toll on the components, and reliability was the worst of any armored German vehicle of the war, with engines, transmissions, steering, everything breaking down rather quickly; it also meant that the tank used gasoline prodigiously, at a time when it was running out in the German inventory. Add to that few roads that could carry this weight, and virtually no bridge in either Germany or France. And finally, the fact that the Germans had to stop production lines making better tanks to produce only a few of these monsters; in fact, only seventy-nine were ever made, all of them issued to just two combat units on the Western Front. Some of these never even made it to the front lines, because it took too much effort to transport these monsters amid Allied bombing raids. Not that great a vehicle after all, once one looks more closely.

But the Germans did, in fact, build a superb tank destroyer. It was called the Jagdpanther.

JAGDPANTHER

Jagdpanther (photo by author,
U.S. Army Ordnance Museum, Aberdeen Proving Ground)

If the Jagdpanther was better than the Jadgtiger, that makes sense, as it was based on the better parent vehicle. Taking the Panther's chassis, steering, powertrain, and lower hull, German engineers built a new superstructure made of sloped 80 mm armor by simply extending the Panther's hull front and side plates upward, and put in the long (L/71) 88 mm cannon of the Tiger II.

The result was a heavy, graceful vehicle that could do everything it was called on to accomplish. Weighing forty-six tons— about the same as a Panther—and with the same engine, the Jagdpanther could easily do 28 mph without the strain of heavier vehicles like the Tiger II. The gun was one of the best ever fielded in the war and could handle just about any Allied tank; on July 30, 1944 three Jagdpanthers wiped out an entire squadron of British

Churchill tanks, which had thicker frontal armor than the Sherman. Fortunately for the Allies, only 392 of these top German tank destroyers were ever made.

A lot of writers love this vehicle, leading to comments like, "The Jagdpanther was one of those vehicles where superlatives could be justifiably lavished, for it was a superb fighting vehicle. . . . it had about it a definite aura that distinguished it from all its contemporaries." Forty, on the other hand, qualified things just a trifle, writing in two separate books that it was "probably the best tank destroyer of the war."[26]

Forty was right to hesitate, because the Jagdpanther, as superb as it was (and it truly was that good), still does not reign as the best tank destroyer of the war. That honor goes to the Russian SU-100.

SU-100

Let's start with some basics: the SU-100 was based on the T-34/85 chassis, in an attempt to mount a larger gun than would be possible in a turreted vehicle. As the title implies, it had a 100 mm gun, a version of a high-velocity naval cannon, in a ball mounting. This was the gun originally contemplated for the JS-II, but not available

SU-100 (photo by author, U.S. Army Ordnance Museum, Aberdeen Proving Ground)

in sufficient numbers. Tank destroyers were secondary weapons in the Russian forces, however, so numbers were not as big a concern, nor was the timing of introduction to the battlefield; the SU-100 arrived in late 1944, months after the JS-II was already at work.

Let's move to the comparison, starting with the all-important firepower. The Jagdpanther's 88 mm L/71's standard armor-piercing round weighed 22 pounds and could penetrate 165 mm of steel plate at 30 degrees at 1,000 meters; if the rare tungsten-core round (lighter, at only 16 pounds) could be found, this went up to 193 mm. Because we are going to need them in a second, the comparable figures for 500 meters are 185 mm and 217 mm, respectively. The SU-100's 100 mm L/54 gun, on the other hand, using the standard armor piercing round at 34 pounds, could handle 150 mm of plate at 30 degrees at 500 meters, as good as the standard German round at that distance. If the Russians used their Arrowhead penetrator, 21 pound round, however—which was *not* that rare—performance went up to 185 mm at 1,000 meters. But because this is at 0 degrees, it is hard to do a precise, direct comparison. It is fair to report, however, based on this data, that both guns were of fairly equal power and able to vanquish the armored enemies of the other side.

If the guns were about the same, so was the armor protection: the Jagdpanther's front plate was 80 mm thick, the SU-100's was 75 mm, at roughly the same angle. Regarding speed, again, there seems to be a similarity, but it is hard to be sure. All sources list the Jagdpanther as being capable of 28 mph, while the SU-100 is listed, depending on the source, as moving from anywhere between 28 and 35 mph.

Thus, we have to turn to other areas to differentiate between the two. The Jagdpanther had better self-protection in that it carried a machine gun to fight infantry, while the SU-100 had none. The Jagdpanther also carried a lot more rounds, sixty compared to the SU-100's thirty-four.

In contrast to this, the SU-100 excelled when it came to reliability and availability/production, not surprising, given the parent vehicles. The Jagdpanther was based on the relatively troubled Panther and started wallowing in problems after 500 miles of travel; after 600 it required a total overhaul. To get to the gearbox, furthermore, you had to remove the entire gun and cradle, an incredible obstacle to fast or easy maintenance. In comparison, the SU-100 derived from one of the most reliable and easily produced armored vehicles of the war, which meant that they stayed in service an awful lot longer, and that there were a lot more of them: 1,675 produced during the war, compared to only 392 for the Jagdpanther, or more than four times as many.[27]

Finally, the SU-100 had it all over the Jagdpanther in one other crucial design element. The German tank destroyer weighed forty-six tons compared to the Russian's thirty-two, and all that weight had to go somewhere.

Most writers comment on how low the Jagdpanther was, because it was almost a foot shorter than the Panther, at eight feet, eleven inches. This seems like a fair thing to applaud, as it means the tank destroyer was less of a target than the tank.

But if that holds true, then compare the SU-100, which stood seven feet, six inches tall, a decrease of almost a foot-and-a-half. That is a lot, and it can be considered in this way: I am five feet, eight inches tall. I have pictures of me (not used here) standing next to an SU-100 at Aberdeen Proving Ground show the top of my head about three-quarters of the way up, toward the top of this vehicle. When I stood next to a Jagdpanther, however, the photo showed it towering over me dramatically, as I barely manage to reach much past half this one's height.[28]

In combat, this was a crucial difference. Without a rotating turret, without the speed of the Hellcat, Russian and German tank destroyers had to depend on using the countryside for cover, so they could bring their firepower to bear before they were spotted and destroyed by more mobile forces. In this kind of warfare, the SU-100 was a much more difficult weapon to spot and hence kill.

The Jagdpanther and the SU-100 compared. Ed Heasley, curator of the
U.S. Army Ordnance Museum, is five feet, ten inches tall.
(photos by author, U.S. Army Ordnance Museum, Aberdeen Proving Ground)

Life is funny. Robert Cortese, writing in *Military Vehicles*, admitted that while the 88 mm L/71 was superior to any tank or anti-tank gun fielded by the Western Allies, it "was surpassed in the East only by the . . . 100 mm" cannon; nevertheless, he still feels the Jagdpanther was "undoubtedly the best tank hunter of World War II."[29]

I disagree. The SU-100 could hide behind hillocks that would make the Jagdpanther stick out like a big dummy, and it packed roughly the same punch with the same protection in a far more reliable mechanical package. It remained in front-line service with Russian forces until 1957, and was still being used by satellite nations in the Third World as late as the 1970s. Its gun, furthermore, went on to arm the standard Russian tank of the early Cold War era, the T-54/55 series, which was made in the tens of thousands and is still seen all over the globe. All in all, this was the best tank destroyer of World War II.

16

THE 88 MM GUN: WAS IT REALLY THE BEST TANK KILLER OF THE WAR?

IF THE TIGER I is the legendary tank of the war, the 88 mm is the legendary gun: Paul Fussell wrote that it was the most important land weapon of World War II in any category. In every account, there is always the crash of the 88 mms, whether as anti-aircraft, anti-tank, or field artillery. One survey of American soldiers during World War II found they feared this more than any other German weapon. Above all, they are spoken of in revered terms as the most effective tank killers of the war. But were they?

As always, let us reveal our intentions, so as to stay honorable. For the purposes of this book, we are evaluating the 88 mm cannon as an anti-tank weapon, not as an anti-aircraft gun or as a field piece; that is, while we will at times discuss its use in these roles, we will not compare it to, say, any of the Allied field pieces or antiaircraft weapons.

The 88 mm cannon started, as did a great many anti-tank weapons, as a gun designed to shoot down planes; other important cannon that began their careers this way were the Russian 85 mm and the American 90 mm.

88 mm gun. This is the FLAK 18 Model. (photo by author,
U.S. Army Ordnance Museum, Aberdeen Proving Ground)

And there is a good reason for that common origin, as cannon
designed to shoot up tanks and shoot down planes operate much
the same way. Unlike indirect weapons like field artillery, both AT
and AA guns are fired at directly sighted targets. More important,
however, those targets are both moving, often as fast as possible.
That means that the preferred weapon must fire a round at very
high velocity, which gives height for anti-aircraft shooting, and a
flat, accurate trajectory when used in the anti-tank mode, as well
as high kinetic energy. In both cases, it also minimizes lead time.

The 88 mm had been in production since 1933 in the anti-
aircraft role, and the standard versions were the Models 18, 36, and
37; variations between these are relatively minor, such as different barrel mountings, carriages, or fire controls. All of these, however, had the same firing characteristics, so they can be treated as
a whole.

How good were these 88 mms? With an L/56 barrel, firing a
21-pound round at 2,600 fps, it could penetrate 105 mm at 30
degrees at 1,000 meters range. Not bad, especially in the early years

of World War II, when tank armor was only 25 to 40 mm thick. As Ian Hogg puts it, "what it could see, it could kill." Period, at least in those days.[30]

But days like that did not last long in the middle of war, as technology rockets ahead in the face of combat. In 1943, the Germans introduced the PAK 43, whose title alone signified how important the anti-tank role had become: previously 88 mms were referred to as FLAK, short for "flugabwehrkanone," or army cannon, and were designed to be used against flying enemies. Anti-aircraft guns, in other words. PAK stands, instead, for "panzerab-wehrkanone," cannon used against armor, or antitank guns.

This PAK 43 was a dilly. With an L/71 barrel, this could get through 167 mm of armor at 30 degrees at 1,000 meters, 192 mm if you used the tungsten-cored shot, although this lost accuracy fast after 500 meters. Many people consider this the best anti-tank gun of the war.

Pretty formidable, but how do both the Models 18/36/37 and the PAK 43 fare when we stack them against some Allied guns? We have already claimed that the 88 mm L/71 gun on the Jagdpan-ther (the equivalent of the PAK 43) was closely matched by the SU-100, but what about the weapons of the Western Front?

The Americans, for example, produced a 90 mm L/50 gun that hurled a 23.4-pound shell at 2,700 fps, or a bigger shell, faster than the Models 18/36/37 could manage. This translated in turn into 109 mm of penetration at 1,000 yards, better than the early 88 mms, but not as good as the PAK 43. Even when the Americans developed a tungsten cored round that could go through 173 mm of plate at 1,000 yards, this remained true.

17-POUNDER ANTI-TANK GUN

It took the British to come up with something finer, and that was the 17-pounder. This translates to roughly 77 mm, but the round had enormous velocity. Using the standard armor-piercing shell, the 17-pounder could handle 188 mm of armor at 30 degrees at 1,000 yards, but it really came into its own in August 1944, when discarding sabot ammunition was provided. With this ammunition, the figure goes up to 231 mm, or substantially more—almost 1.5 inches—than the PAK 43 could do at its best. It was, after all, a 17-pounder-equipped Sherman Firefly that knocked out Michael Wittman's Tiger and killed the great tank ace. Add to that the fact that the standard gun weighed only 4,600 pounds, compared to between 8,000 and 9,700 pounds for the PAK 43 (depending on mounting), and you have a gun that was a deuce of a lot easier to get into and out of position, no small issue to soldiers who have to deal with these beasts.

This was an important difference. One of the leading experts on the 88 mm said it lacked most of the characteristics required for a useful anti-tank gun, including maneuverability, low silhouette, and ease of handling. Even the FLAK 18 was six feet, eleven inches tall and required a nineteen-by-seventeen-foot pit for concealment, an awful lot of work for a gunnery crew, compared to the approximately four-foot-tall British gun that had only modest trail sections to be dealt with. Clearly, the 17 pounder was lighter, handier, and gave better performance than the best of the 88 mms. That makes it a winner, right?

Yes, but I'll qualify that just a tad in a second. First, in order to make sense of that qualification, I want to explain why the 88 mm was such a big deal, because it was.

WHY THE 88 MM WORKED

The real story of the 88 mm's success is the same as that of German tanks, in that the brilliance was in the tactical use, as much as, or even more than in the qualities of the weapon itself. To understand just how successful, how important the 88 mm was, consider the fact that anti-tank guns come in generations. When the war started, for example, every nation employed an anti-tank gun in roughly the 37 to 40 mm range, including the identical German and American 37 mms (the Americans copied the German gun exactly) and the British 2 pounder, or 40 mm, the best of this group. When these would no longer suffice, armies started to field weapons in the 50 to 57 mm range. After that came the 75 mm or so guns, such as the American 75 mm anti-tank gun, the German 75 mm, and the Russian 76.2 mm. Finally, by the end of the war, the standard weapon being fielded was in the 85 to 90 mm range, such as the Russian 85 mm, the German 88 mm, and the American 90 mm.

The Germans, instead, changed the nature of anti-tank warfare when they started using the 88 mm against the Russians and in the desert campaigns, when everybody else was way, way down the evolutionary ladder, still in the 37 to 40 mm stage. By employing the 88 mm so early, in other words, the Germans skipped three generations ahead in one fell swoop, which is more than enough to make anyone dizzy, or in this case, to totally, completely overpower one's opponents. Thus the 88 mm's fearsome reputation.

This really was tactical brilliance. The Americans had the 90 mm early in the war, but refused to use it as an antitank weapon until the last stages, while the Germans had begun experimenting with the 88 mm back during the Spanish Civil War from 1936 to 1939. Even worse were the British, whose 3.7-inch antiaircraft gun was roughly comparable to the 88 mm, and what makes this even sadder, they had more of them than the Germans did their weapon. But during the desert campaigns, when the Germans casually lowered the muzzles of their anti-aircraft guns and found, voila, they could blow away anything that moved through the sands, the British officers adamantly refused to do anything of the kind, since this was an antiaircraft gun, and that, simply and finally, was that. On one occasion, when four 3.7-inch guns stood available to deal with the Afrika Corps, the general in charge had them moved so that they would not get in the way! Similarly, the American 90 mm gun was never adequately employed. Hans Halberstadt, in *The*

World's Great Artillery, said it was "technically superior" to the 88 mm, but, "While the U.S. 90mm AA guns were restricted to guarding port facilities in North Africa, the Germans put the 88 out in the desert where it could engage both tanks and aircraft."[31]

Thus, the immense tactical flexibility of the 88 mm raises questions as to which was best. If it stood higher and weighed a lot more than the 17 pounder, that was in part because it was mounted on a platform that provided 360-degree rotation, as well as total elevation, something no other anti-tank gun could manage, with their fixed carriage and mounts that permitted only a few degrees of movement to either side, before the crew had to manhandle it into another position, hardly something anyone wanted to do in the midst of a tank battle.

The 88 mm, on the other hand, could do most things pretty darn well.[32] General George Marshall, Chief of Staff of the U.S. Army, wrote that the German 88 mm was "ahead of ours in quantity and technique almost to the end of the war." If the American's 90 mm gun had better velocity, it "had no such flexibility. It could not be depressed low enough for effective antitank fire." Furthermore, "interchangeable ammunition was [not] available to the gun when it was needed, and we did not have the numbers of the weapons the Germans had." Or, as Hogg put it, "the potency of the 88 was that it was present, in reasonable numbers, when it was needed. 'They' had them, 'we' didn't. And anything an enemy has which makes life unpleasant for you tends to earn a larger-than-life reputation."[33]

When it comes to the best anti-tank gun of World War II, I stand by my previous judgment: it was the 17 pounder. But overall, the best artillery piece of the war remains the 88 mm.

17

THE BEST
SCIENCE-FICTION TANK
OF THE WAR

ONE OF MY FRIENDS is a comic book artist and writer, who always said that tanks should look like what they really are: giant mechanical monsters of war. He felt that they should appear as if they had jumped out of a Jules Verne or an H. G. Wells novel, and in truth, he captured the vision of what it must have been like for those German soldiers who first saw these creatures lumbering forward on the battlefields of World War I, and then fled in abject panic.

Of all the tanks ever fielded, I think the ones that best personified this esthetic were the multi-turreted devices that had a bit of a vogue in the 1920s and 1930s. The concept here was to turn the tank into a kind of land battleship, to have it fight the way a ship did, with guns blazing in all directions, knocking out a variety of targets simultaneously, which seems like a pretty grand feat indeed, and definitely a war-winner. Maybe.

Give me a second to explain the "maybe," but first, in all fairness, I have to make clear that almost all the major tank-designing powers tried this idea on for size. The British started it all with the

Vickers Independent, which had a tall central turret with a three-pounder gun surrounded by four shorter turrets at every point of the compass, each armed with a machine gun. Even the Germans dabbled with the concept, producing in the pre–Panzer Mk I days a series of experiments labeled "Grosstraktor," each of which had the World War I–era rhomboidal shape, surmounted by a turret with a 75 mm gun, with a separate turret in the back with a machine gun to cover the rear. This was followed in the 1930s by a concept tank that featured multiple turrets, one with the main gun, plus two more with machine guns, this time up front.

But all of these plans went by the wayside, and for good reason. The armies of both these nations quickly realized just what an impossible ideal the multi-turreted tank was, since a commander in a single-turreted tank has more than his hands full. He has to simultaneously pick out targets, direct the driver, keep aware of the rest of the battlefield, align himself with his unit's own attack, follow orders from above, and keep up with his army's larger battle plan. Asking him to also direct a series of additional auxiliary turrets is a design for failure; no one ever could, or ever will be able to handle a task like that, which means you basically have a tank in which most of the crew is undirected, at best at cross purposes, at worst in a state of chaos.

All that did not deter the Russians in the least, however, so they fielded the T-35, the only multi-turreted tank to ever see extensive combat.

This was some tank. First of all, it was absolutely huge, almost 32 feet long and 11.25 feet high; just by means of comparison on that last figure, the King Tiger itself is only 10.75 feet tall, and it is a very, very big vehicle. Put another way, it was 6 feet, 6 inches just to the top of the track guards, making it virtually impossible to get into the thing without a special ladder or outside assistance. This ridiculous height also meant that if the tank was hit, crew members had to exit from the top hatches, eleven feet off the ground, making them lovely targets indeed.

Regarding the length, place it against that of an M4 Sherman, which was only 19.2 feet long, which means that the T-35 was starting to approach the span of two Sherman tanks! Pictures of soldiers standing next to, or on top of these giants are astounding, and one of the best ways to grasp just how immense they really were.[34]

As the T-35 went out into battle, it was gloriously armed, at least if you wanted an image to draw comic books from. In the center, raised above anything else, was a central turret with a very short barrelled 76.2 mm L/16.5 gun that was designed to obliterate fortifications. Below that were four turrets, ringed around the main column. In alternating fashion, they carried two high velocity anti-armor weapons (originally 37 mm but in later models 45 mm), and two 7.62 mm machine guns. There was a crew of eleven men, about the same size as a full infantry squad, and it is hard to imagine that anybody ever did—or ever could—wield them into a fighting unit, a requirement further complicated by the little fact that all these fighting compartments were separated from one another by steel plate. You had to exit the entire vehicle just to go from one turret to another, so one historical account of the T-35 referred to "the commander's total inability to command the tank in combat."

Not many T-35s were made—just fifty-nine of all models—but they were used, both in the war with Finland and during the opening days of Barbarossa. To say that they were a disaster is to risk tragic understatement. Despite weighing 50 tons and having a top speed of 18 mph, their armor was ridiculously thin, no more than 30 mm on the glacis, and an unbelievable 20 mm on the front of the main turret. After that it got thinner, down to 11 mm, which meant the secondary turrets could do little more than stop minor small arms fire and shell fragments. Add to that mechanical components that could not stand the strain of that much weight and broke down, and the fact that they got stuck quite easily,* and,

---

*One Russian commander said the T-35 could not cross large puddles.

because they could not flee in the early days of the Germans' lightning moves, ran out of gas and were abandoned. And, oh yes, because of the command problem, all they did anyway was blunder all over the battlefield. The Germans called them *"kinderschreke,"* toys to frighten children.

But they looked great!

18

THE BIGGEST MONSTERS
OF THE WAR

BY THE END OF THE WAR, monster tanks were coming back in vogue; albeit with only one turret, and often not even that. The Germans take the cake in this competition, and we'll settle their hash in a moment on this score, but in all fairness they were really not alone.

The Americans, for example, actually built what can only be described as a modern-day counterpart of the ancient Roman siege engines, the T28. This was a giant machine that mounted a 105 mm L/67 gun in a ball mount in the front, with no turret at all. Frontal armor was 292 mm thick (almost 12 inches of plate), and it weighed 90 tons. Alas, it used the same engine as the M26 Pershing, which was only half as heavy, so road speed was limited to 8 mph. The idea was to wobble this up to the fortifications of the Siegfried Line and let it whale away, but of the five ordered and two built, none of them arrived in time to see the end of the war. Soon after, the project fell apart, not surprisingly since it no longer had any target that matched its prowess, and since the Army did not even know what to call it; tanks after all, they felt, had turrets, while self-propelled guns had relatively weak armor, and the T28 did not fit either stipulation. Eventually, only one survived, but it was left out in a field to rot for years before it was finally recognized and recovered as a true oddity of the war. Right now it is prominently displayed on a pedestal in front of the Patton Tank Museum at Fort Knox.

The British, furthermore, were not that far behind in this contest. Their idea was the A39 Tortoise, which again put a large gun—in this case, a 32-pounder, or 93 mm—in a rotating mount in the glacis, protected by 225 mm (9 inches) of armor. This little hotrod, however, had a somewhat more powerful engine than the American entry, and at only 87 tons, it could shimmy around the battlefield at the hot pace of 12 mph. For some reason unknown to saner minds, the British actually believed that this could be used as a tank destroyer against foes like the King Tiger.

But as mentioned, the Germans made all these designs look like pikers. The most famous of their planned projects was the Maus, a 150 ton vehicle that would have had frontal armor of 200 mm, with 240 mm on the turret, mounting either a 150 mm gun or the Jagdtiger's 128 mm as primary armament. The coaxial gun, by the way, instead of a machine gun (perish the thought) was a 75 mm cannon, capable of firing fifteen rounds a minute, to be used for lesser targets, like Sherman tanks!

That wasn't the biggest project on the German drawing boards, however, not by a long shot. There was, for example, the little project code-named "Ratte" (Rat). This was a 1,000 ton tank that made the Maus look like, well, a mouse, that would have stretched 35 meters in length (i.e., a tank that was more than a third of a football field long) and 11 meters high, or about that of a 3-story building. Proposed armament was a turret with two 280 mm guns (yes, that is the size of the gun, not the thickness of the armor), in a turret taken from the Graf Spee class battlecrusier, but with the center gun removed.

After that comes the pick of the litter, my personal favorite. This 1,500 ton machine was supposed to be powered by four U-Boat engines, and carry into battle—somehow—an 800 mm gun

with two, minor 150 mm guns in support. One of the lesser problems, by the way, was that in the only available drawing it appears
to have had an extremely high center of gravity, which made it
highly subject to keeling over! Albert Speer dubbed this project
"Monster," and he was being kind.

19

THE BEST HALF-TRACK

THE ORIGIN OF THE HALF-TRACK actually came in Russia, but by way of French know-how. In 1910, French-born Adolph Kegresse was manager of the Czar's garage, and he came up with the idea of replacing the back wheels of several cars, including Packards and Rolls Royces, with a simple track and bogie system in order to better navigate the snow-bound roads of Mother Russia. During the Revolution Kegresse wisely ducked out, landing first in Finland, then returning to his French homeland. There he began to be associated with the Citroen firm, and in 1923 its reputation became established when five Citroen half-tracks became the first motorized vehicles to make it across the Sahara Desert.

After that, however, most of the nations of the world lost interest, even though they had been experimenting with this new form of vehicle fairly widely throughout the 1920s. By the mid-1930s, for example, the British, in fact, had totally lost interest, and later on, during the war, very few of the great powers—not even Russia, a nation that did so well with armored designs—ever came up with much in the way of half-tracks.

The leader in the field, therefore, became Germany, and for good reason. Blitzkrieg tactics had dictated that there had to be some fast, at least lightly armored means of moving the troops of the panzer divisions, so that they could keep up with the slashing attacks. But that also meant having a vehicle with superior off-road ability compared to a truck, something that could keep up with, and possibly even fight alongside of the tanks.

The first answer they had was to give each division a battalion of men equipped with motorcycles and sidecars, but while that may have provided speed, mobility over rough terrain was severely limited. So as an alternative, they began to field a large number of different half-tracks, covering every role from artillery-hauler to armored personnel carrier.

SDKFZ 251

Though we will mention the former in a moment, it is primarily the latter models that concern us here, as they were the core of the fighting use of the half-track in every army. And for this purpose, the Germans' best effort was the SdKfz 251 (SdKfz stands for "Sonderkraftfahrzeug," or special-purpose vehicle, and it was used to designate a variety of fighting types, not just half-tracks, but armored cars as well).

SdKfz 251 half-track (photo by author,
U.S. Army Ordnance Museum, Aberdeen Proving Ground)

In truth, this should more accurately be referred to as a "three-quarter track," given how far the treads extend along the body; the front axle, however, was unpowered, a telling point. Armor plating was minor, only 14.5 mm in the front and 8 mm on the sides, and it had a 100 hp engine that gave it a top speed of 34 mph. It could hold up to a dozen men if you really crammed them in, but if you wanted the troops to fight along the way, eight was a much more realistic figure. In addition, the SdKfz 251 was eventually used to mount just about every weapon possible, from rockets to a huge infrared detection device to be used in conjunction with an infrared searchlight mounted on a Panther; in this guise, it was referred to as the "Uhu," or owl.

It was, as usual for the Germans, the application, more than the weapon, that was revolutionary. The idea of moving infantry in a semi-tracked vehicle along with the tanks was a novel one. If at first the SdKfz 251 was perceived by the Germans as a battle taxi, they soon discovered that the reality of combat had turned it into a fighting vehicle in its own right, as soldiers leaned over the sides and poured out fire against the enemy.

This was a superb innovation, and as such, it caught the attention of other counties. Only the United States did anything about it, however, in part because it had the automotive manufacturing capacity to experiment with new ideas.

M3/M5

Their product was the M3/M5 series of half-tracks (the numbers only designate different manufacturers), which is the only other vehicle in the same league as the SdKfz 251. Let's see how they compare.

Frankly, in just about every aspect, the M3 series beats the German models. First of all, they were longer, although that does not seem as obvious when one looks at the long, lean 251 with its

M5 half-track (photo by author at Duxford,
UK. Permission by owner of the vehicle.)

extended track: the German vehicle is nineteen feet long, while the
M3 is twenty feet, three inches long. Far more important, however,
the M3 has a considerably larger carrying compartment—the single
most important aspect of a vehicle like this, after all—that gives
20 percent more space than the SdKfz 251. Armor protection was a
bit lower than that on the 251, only 6 mm on the sides and 12 mm
on the front (and straight up, as opposed to a 55 degree angle on
the 251), but given what they were facing, that is not significantly
different from the figures for the German vehicle; neither could stop
much beyond small arms fire. Nevertheless, American soldiers sometimes called them "purple-heart boxes" and kidded that the armor
worked fine; it allowed bullets to come in but not go out the other
side, so that they could rattle around for a while inside the cabin.
The truth was, none of these vehicles were supposed to resist very
heavy fire, and were used to provide a powerful increase in mobility with a modicum of protection, and nothing more.

Where the Americans really excelled over the Germans, however, was in two related areas, automotive qualities and production.

Most Americans who drove both vehicles said that they preferred the M3/M5, and that wasn't just because of familiarity or nationalism. First of all, it had a much more powerful engine, with 147 hp instead of 100, almost a 50 percent increase. This meant a number of things, such as the fact that the M3/M5s could go faster than the 251s, with top speed usually listed as 45 mph (you can actually hit 55 mph), an attribute which the Americans used to the fullest. In small French villages where the Americans feared being ambushed in the narrow streets, they would take a half-track fitted with multiple .50 caliber machine guns (the M16—see the discussion later on), then run it full tilt down the street, shooting up everything on one side. After that they would run it back again, obliterating the other side of the street, a tactic that usually worked to nullify any Germans laying in wait. Someone who drove a restored American half-track wrote it was like handling any other large, modern, four-wheeled drive vehicle, albeit one in which power steering was either absent or had failed (he also notes something nobody talks about in any of the standard works: that light armored vehicles vibrate terribly and make a tremendous clamor as everything rattles around inside).

As for general mobility, this was a mixed bag, but again the American vehicle comes out ahead. The 251 had one ability that the M3/M5 did not, in that it could steer by manipulating relative power to the tracks as well as by turning the front tires, which gave it a superior turning ability in some rough situations. That was matched and beaten, however, by some characteristics of the American series, the most telling of which was that it had a powered front axle. Not only did that give it superior traction in general, it also vastly improved handling. SdKfz 251s were impossible to control in mud or snow, while the powered front wheels of the M3/M5, much like those of a four-wheel drive vehicle today, bit in and held the road. Keep in mind, too, the Americans used wider tracks—crucial to reducing ground pressure; theirs were twelve inches wide, compared to only ten inches on the SdKfz 251. While the German tracks were longer, this at least helped to mitigate that advantage. In addition, it was standard to mount on the front of the American half-tracks either a powered winch to pull out bogged vehicles, or else a roller that enabled them to overcome obstacles that the 251 could not manage.

Beyond that, the usual type of problems that overwhelmed German armored vehicles once more occurred. The SdKfz 251 was constructed much like a tank, and an extremely well-made one at that; it had manganese-steel track shoes and a torsion-bar suspension, while the various armored plates were carefully cut and assembled. The result was a vehicle that took a lot of time and skilled manpower to produce, and was correspondingly expensive; a large German half-track (not the SdKfz 251) cost 60,000 Reichsmarks to produce, compared to 82,500 Reichsmarks for a Sturmgeschutz III assault gun, a fully tracked, fully armored vehicle equipped with a 75 mm gun. In addition, all that quality came with the usual complication, that this vehicle usually required more maintenance than simpler ones, and in consequence, broke down a lot more often.

This, in turn, was complicated by the usual German tendency to tinker, and make a lot more different kinds of vehicles than was really necessary. The Americans built one basic model, then modified it for different roles. The Germans, on the other hand, designed, built, and fielded the widest variety of half-track vehicles imaginable, even when some of these roles could have been handled by only a few different designs. Instead, the variety ranged from the tiny Kettenrad, with a motorcycle front and capable of carrying only two men in the half-track rear, to the Zugkraftwagen 18, a giant designed to haul large artillery pieces and recover other armored vehicles.

The result was that total production of German half-tracks of all kinds, while still in the thousands, lagged way behind the Americans' ability to turn out 41,470 half-tracks during the war. This, in turn, had enormous ramifications, since it meant that the Americans and not the Germans became the first to totally mechanize their armies, the first to really engage in this kind of warfare in its fullest realization. In general, at their best, only one out of four infantry battalions in the German panzer divisions rode in armored personnel carriers of any sort, the rest following up in standard commercial trucks or even worse, on foot. The Americans, on the other hand, pioneered in equipping every infantry unit in the armored divisions with sufficient half-tracks to carry all of their members, something no other army came close to achieving, which gave them an enormous edge when it came to tactical mobility.

This, in turn, combined with the flexibility of the M3/M5 series

M16 half-track with quad .50 caliber mount
(Robert Bruce Military Photo Features)

to mount a variety of weapons and accessories. The best of these was the M16, which mounted a Maxson turret with four .50 caliber M2 machine guns and which had electronically driven traverse and elevation. Originally designed as an anti-aircraft weapon, it proved to be a devastating ground attack system, one that could decimate enemy infantry as few other weapons could, either before or since.

This flexibility, combined with speed, reliability, and numbers, made the American half-tracks the best of the war.

20

THE BEST
ARMORED CAR

UNLIKE THE CASE WITH HALF-TRACKS, every nation made armored cars, and for good reason. All technologically advanced nations built automobiles in those days, and it did not take much to mount some armor on an overloaded chassis, add a machine gun, and send the ensuing product out to the battlefield. That approach, however, does not a war-winner make, and sooner or later some factories started to design and build weapons platforms designed for the job. Of these, the products of two nations stand out.

Once again, we are posing Americans versus Germans, but in this case the winner is not that clear cut. Part of this was because the Germans understood how to use these vehicles better: they understood that while the armored car was no tank, a good, lightly armored and armed vehicle could do superb reconnaissance work. German officers felt that for this kind of mission, mobility counted more than anything, and the most important attribute, next to that, was a good radio; as one German recon officer put it, "The best patrols I had were those with clean guns." The Americans, on the other hand, never fully accepted this concept, feeling that it could better be accomplished by slower, but better protected and more capable light tanks; one of their training manuals explained, "the light tank company . . . may be used to exploit the success of the medium tank [companies], to execute battle reconnaissance, or to act as a covering force for the [tank] battalion." At the end of the war, the U.S. military totally eliminated armored cars from its Table of Organization, at a time when many other nations, including Britain and France, continued developing the type.[35]

AMERICAN ARMORED CARS

The American story is much more complicated, because its best armored car never got into production. This was a vehicle with six wheels evenly spaced, featuring cross country mobility far superior to the M8 already in production. But the design—tentatively called the M38 Wolfhound—came too late for the war, and as noted, the U.S. didn't like armored cars anyway, and wanted to phase them out.

Instead, the standard American armored cars of World War II were the M8/M20 series, which used the same chassis and components but with different upper structures. In its initial form, the M8 had a 110 hp engine that enabled it to zip along at 55 mph on six wheels, unevenly distributed with two sets in the rear and one set in the front. Armor was no more than 20 mm on the front, and half that on the sides. It mounted a turret with a 37 mm cannon and a coaxial .30 caliber machine gun, with a .50 caliber Browning on a pedestal at the rear to defend against air attacks, although it was probably used a lot more against infantry and other ground targets. The M20, on the other hand, was essentially the same machine, but with the turret removed, replaced by a ring-mounted .50 caliber and with more room for personnel or matériel. Both of these vehicles, unfortunately, continued the American tradition of having wide-open, unarmored tops, letting in grenades, shellbursts, and even the rain.

M8 armored car. In World War II, there would have been a
.50 caliber machine gun mounted atop the turret. (photo by author,
American Society of Military History Military Museum, South El Monte, CA)

In action, the M8s and M20s were handy little vehicles, although the American command never appreciated them. A recent driver of a restored M20 reported that the ride was strikingly smooth, even when it went over rough farm terrain or surmounted railroad tracks; on good roads, it felt like a standard automobile. One former commander of a cavalry troop, General William Knowlton (ret.), told how he actually knocked out a Panther with an M8 by hitting it in the rear, a lucky shot that few would try and repeat and fewer would survive. He did make the point, however, that these wheeled vehicles were quiet (recon units in jeeps "could hear the leaves rustle" he claimed), something no longer true once treads replaced tires in the reconnaissance mission. "Never again would mounted scouts have sensitive hearing unmarred by vehicle and track noise," he wrote, a statement that is perceptive but no longer totally accurate, as army scouts now use HUMVEEs extensively.[36]

Actually, the best American armored car design never got built. The M8's wheel layout, with one axle in the front, separated by considerable space from the two axles in the rear, prevented it from crossing any kind of substantial trench. To overcome this, designers produced a vehicle with six evenly spaced wheels and oversized tires that could pass over a 50-inch-wide hole in the ground. The body was better shaped, with better sloped armor, but alas, once again the turret had an open roof; some things never change, it seems. But by this time, the end of the war was in sight, and the Army, recognizing that it had enough vehicles for present and future needs and phasing out armored cars anyway, refused to order production. The British, on the other hand, took a good close look, and there are a great many similarities between this design (known as the M38 Wolfhound), and their Saladin, one of the best armored cars of the postwar era.

234/2 Puma

In contrast to this approach, the Germans reveled in armored car designs of all kinds: four wheeled, six wheeled, and up. Of these, far and away the best were the eight-wheeled vehicles.

All the models in this last series, known as the SdKfz 234s, were powered by a 200 hp diesel engine that gave the vehicle a 53 mph top speed, with power and steering in all eight tires. This, in turn, meant they had excellent traction in the worst climates, almost as good, in fact, as treaded vehicles, and they excelled in the mud of the Russian front. They could also be driven as fast in reverse as in forward, a handy feature for a reconnaisance vehicle that was supposed to pull out, avoid combat, and report back in the minimal time. Armor ranged from 30 mm in the front to 8 mm side hull plates at 55 degrees.

Most of these had open-topped superstructures, but on one model they added a turret (amazingly enough, with a roof this time!), and by the time they had finished they had created a masterpiece. This model was designated the 234/2, but it is always referred to as the Puma, although that nickname was never official during the war, unlike the cat titles given tanks.

This Puma had claws, too, since it mounted a long barreled 50 mm L/60 gun with a coaxial 7.92 mm machine gun, enough firepower to take on anything but a medium tank, and far more than any other armored car and even most light tanks. The gun fired a round at 2,700 fps, which could puncture 59 mm of armor at 500 meters, and was generally more accurate than even the Panzer Mk IV's 75 mm.

Like the T-34, however, there is something about the Puma that goes beyond simple specifications. It remains one of the most graceful military vehicles ever built, with a brilliance of line that few have ever come close to. Combine that sheer beauty with superior mobility and firepower, and nothing comes close.

With one qualification. While there is no question in my mind that, one-on-one, the Puma was the best armored car of the war, there is another little matter that sticks in my craw. Although the Germans made over 2,300 vehicles when one looks at the entire 234 series, their total production of the Puma, which did not hit the battlefield until mid-1944, was a minuscule 101.

Therein lies the problem. It is really hard to give credit to something that barely appeared in combat, while the United States produced 11,667 M8s and another 3,791 M20s. Simply put, these towering numbers mean that the American vehicle, while not as good, played a far more important role on the battlefield.

The more things change . . . the more we still try and make sense out of them.

POSTSCRIPT:
IT'S YOUR TURN!

THERE'S AN awful lot of data in this book—facts, descriptions, and photos, not to mention my own finicky judgments. Where should the reader go from here?

Well, you could take the book and just throw it in the can, but there's a better idea. As mentioned in the introduction, I hope things don't end here; in fact, they should start. My own suggestion is to simply think about what you've read. Take some time, roll it around in your mind, and then reach your own darn conclusions. What do you think should be named the best rifle, tank, and so on, and why?

Even better, pass the book along to a buddy, then afterward sit down over pizza, coffee, or whatever and argue for your choices. Let each other know that Slayton is just a blowhard, and how much smarter you are than that so-called author.

But for my two cents, here's what I think you should really do. Go out and actually talk to some World War II vets. Ask them what they used and how it worked. Did they like it or not, and why? What did they hear about other weapons? Then ask them about the rest of their experiences in the war. Believe me, you'll be fascinated.

Finding World War II vets is easy enough. More often than not, they're the grandfather of someone down the block. Or just look up veterans' organizations in your local phone directory or on the

Web. You'll be surprised at how many are around, and what they have to say.

In my mind, that would be the most rewarding outcome of this book. Talking to a vet is like stretching out your hand to touch a piece of the past. It's a time machine that takes you past intellect and helps you feel and understand—with your gut and your heart— what that era was really like. One of the joys of my life has been talking to these men and women whenever I could, as well as reading their words.

My only other suggestion would be to move fast, for we are losing that generation every day, and they are a special group. For a discussion like this, the most special of all.

NOTES

PART I: INFANTRY WEAPONS

1. John Nalis, "A Company Commander's Thoughts on Iraq," *Armor* (January–February 2004), p. 13.
2. In some circles, this is known as a "New York reload."
3. Timothy Mullin, *Handbook of Handguns* (Boulder, CO: Paladin Press, 2002), pp. 83, 88.
4. This account comes from Edward Ezell, *Handguns of the World* (Harrisburg, PA: Stackpole Books, 1981).
5. Bruce Canfield, *U.S. Infantry Weapons of World War II* (Lincoln, RI: Andrew Mowbray Publications, 1994), p. 54.
6. The Astra firm in Spain actually made blowback pistols using powerful cartridges, the Models 400 in 9 mm Largo and 600 in 9 mm Parabellum, respectively. But in order to do this, they employed very, very heavy recoil springs, making them a veritable bear to cock.
7. *Gun Tests* (November 2002), p. 12.
8. One indication of the relative recoil forces is by comparing the amount of propellant used in pistol and rifle ammunition. Though there is enormous variance by manufacturer and country, certain generalities still make the point. The 9 mm round, for example, used between 3 and 6 grains of propellant. Compare this to the American .30-06 with 50 grains, the British .303 with 37 grains, and the German 7.92 mm with 45 grains. Actually, the best measurement of how much recoil force—the kick—was muzzle velocity: the 9 mm leaves the barrel with 365 ft/lbs of energy, compared to the .30-06s 2,700 ft/lbs!
9. Hugo Schmeisser actually had nothing to do with the design of the famous World War II submachine guns, the MP.38 and the MP.40, but they were called that at the time, and every action writer still seems to use the term.

10. The Dunlap quotes come from Roy Dunlap, *Ordnance Went Up Front* (Livonia, NY: R&R Books, 1948), p. 58.

11. Various quotes from Mullin on submachine guns come from: Timothy Mullin, *The Fighting Submachine Gun* (Boulder, CO: Paladin Press, 1999).

12. The report read, "This is probably the best 'gangster' weapon we have ever seen."

13. Kevin Smith, *The Owen Gun Files* (Sydney: Turton & Armstrong, 1994), p. 39.

14. Revolver cartridges are rimmed so that they will not slide out of the cylinder; this makes them next to impossible to use in a submachine gun, which depends on rounds sliding easily through a complicated mechanism, and above all, on stacking neatly in the magazine. The army claimed they made the request because they happened to have some .38 caliber revolver ammunition available.

15. The Sten was the standard submachine gun of the British army; naturally, the Australians thought it was the best gun of its kind ever made.

16. The quotes are from Wayne Wardman, *The Owen Gun* (Sydney: n.p., n.d.), pp. 153–154.

17. The Russians made thousands of wooden fighter planes as well; they really did have that much wood.

18. The chrome plating was also important because Russian small arms ammunition used a particularly corrosive primer, because it was cheaper to make and enjoyed a very long shelf life in poor environmental conditions, which meant most of the Soviet Union, most of the time. But with the chromed barrels, you could field strip the gun, rinse the barrel in a local stream or river, and all the chlorate compounds that would foul most other weapons were gone.

19. The quote comes from Robert Bruce, *German Automatic Weapons of World War II* (London: Windrow & Greene, 1996), p. 30.

20. Evgeni Bessonov, *Tank Rider*, translated by Blair Irincheev (London: Greenhill Books, 2003), p. 208.

21. David Bolotin, *Soviet Small-Arms and Ammunition* (Finland: Finnish Arms Museum Foundation, 1995), p. 59.

22. *New York Times*, May 7, 2000.

23. Peter Kokalis, "Yugo Mausers," *Small Arms Review*, 7 (December 2003), p. 48; Timothy Mullin, *Testing the War Weapons* (Boulder, CO: Paladin Press, 1997).

24. Joseph Springer, *The Black Devil Brigade* (Pacifica, CA: Pacifica Military History, 2002), p. 132.

25. E-mail from Edward Rudnicki to H-War, February 9, 2003.

26. The quote comes from Ian Hogg and John Weeks, *Military Small Arms of the 20th Century* (Iola, WI: Krause Publications, 2000), p. 105.

27. Edward Ezell, *The Great Rifle Controversy* (Harrisburg, PA: Stackpole Books, 1984), p. 286.

28. Hogg and Weeks, *Military Small Arms*, p. 7.

29. Belton Cooper, *Death Traps* (Navato, CA: Presidio Press, 1998), p. 144.

30. The stories in this paragraph come from Julian Hatcher, *The Book of the Garand* (Highland Park, NJ: Gun Room Press, 1948).

31. Frank Iannamico, "Ordnance Committee Meeting, 23 December, 1943," *Small Arms Review* 4 (December 2000), pp. 78–79.

32. In one survey of riflemen conducted during the Korean War, 87 percent said virtually all their shots were at targets 300 yards away or less. Most kills, however, occurred at ranges less than 100 yards.

33. Walter Hern, "Kalashnikov vs Sturmgewehr," *Small Arms Review* 3 (July 2000), pp. 54–59.

34. John Walter, *Rifles of the World*, 2nd ed. (Iola, WI: Krause Publications, 1998), p. 176.

35. *Gun Tests* compared the precision of the MG 42 sight to a Leica camera, and called it "the most precisely machined machine gun ever made." *Gun Tests* (July 2003), p. 13.

36. Peter Kokalis, "An MG42/MG3/MG74 Morph", *Small Arms Review* (December 2003), p. 51.

37. The MG 42 was so much cheaper to make than the MG 34, it wasn't funny. The latter cost 310 Reichsmarks to manufacture ($107.30 at then current exchange rates) compared to only 250 RM ($88.25) for the MG 42. Far more important, the 42 cut manufacturing time by an astonishing one-third.

38. Timothy Mullin, *Testing the War Weapons* (Boulder, CO: Paladin Press, 1997), p. 126.

39. The roller lock system was actually created by a Pole, Edward Stacke. In 1939, the German Army grabbed his designs and a prototype after they invaded Poland and incorporated his ideas into their own projects.

40. In all fairness, the recent trend has been to go back to medium and light machine guns. From the very start, critics of the GPMG argued that compromise was the enemy of excellence, that by keeping the

weapons separate, each would be superior to a catch-all concept. Later on, there was the reasonable claim that GPMGs were really not that light, and that a true light machine gun was needed, something far easier to carry about, but still capable of giving the squad sustained firepower.

41. Despite this, the Bren was still cheaper to make than the Lewis, which gives some idea of what it took to turn out those solid World War I weapons.

42. Again, Hogg wrote that the Bren "gained a reputation for reliability never equaled by any other light machine gun before or since." Ian Hogg, *Machine Guns* (Iola, WI: Krause Publications, 2002), p. 115.

43. Some sources say the Bren was actually too accurate, given that a large part of its job was suppressive fire, and it cost a lot of time, money, and effort to make the gun that precise.

44. Roger Ford, *The World's Great Machine Guns* (New York: Barnes and Noble, 1999), p. 86.

45. The Russians also produced a heavy machine gun during World War II for ground use, the Degtyarev. See the discussion later on for their heavy machine gun designed for aircraft use.

46. Cooper, *Death Traps*, p. 62; Gene Gangarosa Jr., *FN . . . Browning* (Wayne, NJ: Stoeger Publishing, 1999), p. 138; John Irwin, *Another River, Another Town* (New York: Random House, 2002, p. 114).

47. John Walter, *Modern Machine-Guns* (London: Greenhill Books, 2000), p. 16.

48. The Russians are still doing this, by the way. Their present-day GSH-301 30 mm aircraft cannon is just as reliable and hard hitting as Western models, but weighs far less.

49. Charles Sharp, *Soviet Infantry Tactics in World War II* (West Chester, OH: George Nofziger, 1998), p. 112; Ian Hogg, *Mortars* (Ramsbury: Crowood Press, 2001), pp. 93–94.

50. Springer, *Black Devil Brigade*, p. 157.

51. Anthony Williams, *Rapid Fire* (Shrewsbury: Airlife, 2000), p. 221.

52. Ian Hogg, *Encyclopedia of Infantry Weapons of World War II* (New York: Bison Books, 1977), p. 149.

53. Harold Leinbaugh and John Campbell, *The Men of Company K* (New York: William Morrow, 1985), p. 258; Cooper, *Death Traps*, p. 186; Michael Green, *M4 Sherman* (Osceola, WI: Motorbooks International, 1993), p. 31.

PART II: TANKS

1. Bryan Perrett, *German Light Panzers* (Oxford: Osprey, 1998), p. 3.

2. Caliber in small arms represents hundredths of an inch; it takes four calibers, thus, to make one millimeter, making a 9 mm round pistol approximately .35 caliber.

3. Bryan Perrett, *Panzerkampfwagen III Medium Tank, 1936–1944* (Oxford: Osprey, 1999), pp. 44–45.

4. Even as late as Kursk in 1943, the Wehrmacht fielded 196 Panthers, 181 Tigers, 615 Mk IVs, and 597 Mk IIIs, out of roughly 2,200 tanks thrown into that battle.

5. Perrett, *Panzerkampfwagen III*, p. 23.

6. George Forty, *German Tanks in World War II* (London: Blandford Press, 1987), p. 90; Robert Crisp, *Brazen Chariots* (New York: Ballantine Books, 1961), p. 69.

7. R. M. Ogorkiewicz, *Armoured Forces* (New York: Arco Publishing, 1970), p. 178.

8. In reality, the true genius of blitzkreig was its use of combined arms tactics. Armies before and now tend to isolate various branches of the service—for example, tankers still shy from training with infantry as equal partners—in order to focus their skills and create espirit de corps. The Germans, on the other hand, melded all forms of firepower into a flowing mass, where each segment complemented the other's shortcomings and protected their weak points. This is still the key to victory today.

9. Forty, *German Tanks*, p. 94. Lloyd George is quoted in Werner Regenberg, *An Illustrated Guide to German Panzers, 1935–1945* (Atglen, PA: Schiffer Military History, 2002), p. 62.

10. David Glantz and Jonathan House, *When Titans Clash* (Lawrence: University Press of Kansas, 1995), p. 10.

11. The Germans were masters at operational warfare, but the Western Allies never could really handle the concept, as they were burdened with a command structure that had to take into account national and personal rivalries, as well as several years less experience in mass warfare. The closest they came was in the Falaise campaign, when they failed to close the gap and allowed tens of thousands of German soldiers to escape, admittedly with a drastic loss of equipment. But that kind of mistake was not being made at all on the Russian front by either side, by that point in the war.

12. Koshkin also suggested the name "T-34"; it memorialized a 1934 state edict vastly expanding the armored forces in the Soviet Union.

13. Richard Humble, *Tanks* (London: Arthur Barker, 1977), pp. 89–90.

14. The Russians also used some interesting expedients to extend range. They found that if they mixed captured German gasoline with kerosene—also abundant, since the Wehrmacht used it as a heating fuel—in a ratio of two parts kerosene to one part gasoline, it would power the T-34's engine. This mixture usually wound up overheating things a bit, but in some cases that was still better than being stuck at a crucial point in a battle.

15. One German general said that his forces "could never assume that the Russians would be held back by terrain normally considered impassable. It was in just such places that his appearance, and frequently, his attack, had to be expected." Erhard Rauss, quoted in Tim Bean and Will Fowler, *Russian Tanks of World War II* (St. Paul, MN: MBI Publishing, 2002), p. 162.

16. Quoted in Steven Zaloga, "Technological Surprise and the Initial Period of War: The Case of the T-34 Tank in 1941," *Journal of Slavic Military Studies* 6 (December 1993), p. 644.

17. Hans Halberstadt, *Inside the Great Tanks* (London: Windrow & Greene, 1997).

18. Hans Halberstadt, *Military Vehicles* (New York: Michael Friedman Publishing Group, 1998), p. 50.

19. Just by means of perspective, in 1975, when the designers were finishing up the first working prototypes of the M1 Abrams, the Cubans were still using T-34/85s in Angola.

20. Steven Zaloga, *Red Army Handbook* (Phoenix Mill, UK: Sutton Publishing, 1998), p. 162; Bryan Perrett, *Soviet Armour* (London: Blandford Press, 1987); p. 17; Humble, *Tanks*, p. 84; Christopher Chant, *Armoured Fighting Vehicles of the 20th Century* (London: Tiger Books International, 1996), p. 106; Chris Ellis and Peter Chamberlain, *The Great Tanks* (London: Hamlyn, 1975), p. 52.

21. This is approximately twenty-two yards, only two downs in an American football game. This is extremely close to be engaging in armored combat in the first place, and even more troublesome when one's shells bounce off at a range at which you could practically hurl them at the enemy.

22. Steven Zaloga, *T-34/75 Medium Tank* (London: Osprey, 1994), pp. 12, 14; Matthew Hughes and Chris Mann, *The T-34 Russian Battle Tank* (Osceola, WI: MBI Publishing Company, 1999), pp. 57, 60; Wolfgang

Fleisher, "Battling the T-34—German Perspective," *Tankograd Gazette*, no. 15 (0), pp. 6–7.

23. Wolfgang Fleisher, *Russian Tanks and Armored Vehicles, 1917–1945* (Atglen, PA: Schiffer Military History, 1999), pp. 141, 143.

24. Hughes and Mann, *T-34*, pp. 60–62.

25. Quoted in Hughes and Mann, *T-34*, p. 57.

26. Senior University of Michigan historian Gerald Linderman argues that the alpha and omega of brutality in the European theater was Russia and North Africa, with the former being the most barbaric, the latter evidenced by the most restrained, or polite warfare seen during World War II in any major battle zone. *The World Within War* (New York: The Free Press, 1997).

27. Tom Jentz and Hilary Doyle, *Tiger I* (London: Osprey, 1993), pp. 3, 7; Wolfgang Fleisher, *The Battle Tank VI "Tiger" with the Troops* (Atglen, PA: Schiffer Military History, 2000), p. 15.

28. Roger Ford, *The Tiger Tank* (Osceola, WI: Motorbooks International, 1998), p. 20.

29. Andrew Hull, David Markov, and Steven Zaloga. *Soviet/Russian Armor and Artillery Design Practices* (Darlington, MD: Darlington Publications, 1999), p. 12.

30. Michael Green, *Tiger Tanks* (Osceola, WI: Motorbooks International, 1995), p. 103.

31. Erik Lund to H-WAR, November 9, 2001.

32. Halberstadt, *Military Vehicles*, p. 66.

33. The Russians found it was much harder to penetrate the front plate of a Panther than that of a Tiger, even though technically the latter had thicker armor in that spot.

34. In all fairness, the Panther's armor got worse during the course of the war, as the Germans ran out of manganese alloy and substituted high-carbon steel with nickel, which was more brittle, especially at the seams.

35. The round used in the 75 mm L/70 was so powerful, the gun could only be fired with the muzzlebrake attached, or it would wreck the tank.

36. John Ellis, *The Sharp End of War* (Newton Abbott, UK: David & Charles, 1980), pp. 128–129.

37. Halberstadt, *Military Vehicles*, p. 68.

38. Roger Ford, *The World's Great Tanks* (New York: Barnes and Noble Books, 1997), p. 51.

39. Peter Gudgin, *Armoured Firepower* (Phoenix Mill, UK: Sutton Publishing, 1997), p. 91.

40. Matthew Hughes and Chris Mann, *The Panther Tank* (Osceola, WI: MBI Publishing, 2000), p. 39.

41. In March 1945, 9,968 people toiled at the Maschinenfabrik Augsberg-Nurnberg AG factories, most of them making Panther tanks. More than half of these employees were foreign workers.

42. Ford, *Tiger Tank*, p. 16.

43. Halberstadt, *Inside the Great Tanks*, p. 79; letter from Marsh Gelbart to the author, August 18, 1998.

PART III: OTHER ARMORED VEHICLES

1. In the first version, of which fifty were made, a Porsche-designed turret had 110 mm of armor set at 60 degrees.

2. Evgeni Bessonov, *Tank Rider* (London: Greenhill Books, 2003), p. 186.

3. Wolfgang Fleisher, *Soviet Tanks and Armored Vehicles, 1917–1945* (Atglen, PA: Schiffer Military History, 1999), p. 156; Steven Zaloga and James Grandsen, *Soviet Heavy Tanks* (London: Osprey, 1981), p. 29.

4. You can try it for yourself at the Ordnance Museum at the Aberdeen Proving Ground.

5. George Forty, *World War II Tanks* (London: Osprey, 1995), p. 120; Christopher Chant, *World Encyclopedia of the Tank* (Somerset: Patrick Stephens, 1994), p. 201.

6. *"Tanks Are Mighty Fine Things"* (Detroit: Chrysler Corporation, 1946), p. 82.

7. Michael Green, *M4 Sherman* (Osceola, WI: Motorbooks International, 1993), p. 76.

8. Michael Green, *Patton's Tank Drive* (Osceola, WI: Motorbooks International, 1995), p. 90; Michael Green, *Tiger Tanks* (Osceola, WI: Motorbooks International, 1995), p. 59; Nat Frankel and Larry Smith, *Patton's Best* (New York: Hawthorne Books, 1978), p. 65.

9. The basic Sherman was 9' tall, the later M4A3E8 ("Easy 8") an amazing 11'3". This compares less than favorably to the 9'7" Tiger and the 9'10" Panther. The Russian T-34, on the other hand, was only 7'10", a much smaller target, and even the Russian's heavy tank, the IS-2, was only 8'11". To put this into perspective, the M1A1 Abrams is only 9'6" tall!

10. The McNeese quote is in Joseph Springer, *The Black Devil Brigade* (Pacifica, CA: Pacifica Military History, 2001), p. 208; the German quote comes from Gerald Linderman, *The World Within War* (New York: The Free Press, 1997), pp. 25–26.

11. Frankel and Smith, *Patton's Best*, p. 137. In actuality, studies have shown that more Shermans were lost to ammunition fires than anything else. Hot shards from an antitank round would penetrate the brass casings and start a fire in the propellant, which took only about thirty seconds before the other rounds lit up. The inside of the Sherman then became an inferno, and the fire could continue for a day or longer.

12. Green, *M4 Sherman*, p. 34.

13. David Johnson, *Fast Tanks and Heavy Bombers* (Ithaca, NY: Cornell University Press, 1998), p. 185.

14. Quoted in Green, *M4 Sherman*, p. 102.

15. *New York Times*, March 18, 1945.

16. *New York Times*, March 19, 1945.

17. Belton Cooper, *Death Traps* (Navato, CA: Presidio Press, 1998), p. vii.

18. The two best books to examine the tank destroyer doctrine, its failure and effect on American tank development, and its use in World War II, are Charles Baily, *Faint Praise* (Hamden, CT: Archon Books, 1983) and Johnson, *Fast Tanks*.

19. Johnson, *Fast Tanks*, pp. 192, 193.

20. Baily, *Faint Praise*, p. 35.

21. Taylor Downing and Andrew Johnson, *Battle Stations* (Barnsley, UK: Pen and Sword Books, 2000), p. 151.

22. Mark Hayward, *Sherman Firefly* (Essex, UK: Barbarossa Books, 2001), p. 148.

23. Green, *Patton's Tank Drive*, p. 92.

24. Jim Winchester, *The World War II Tank Guide* (Edison, NJ: Chartwell Books, 2000), p. 49.

25. George Forty, *German Tanks of World War II "In Action"* (London: Blandford Press, 1987), p. 141.

26. Chris Bishop, ed., *The Encyclopedia of Weapons of World War II* (New York: Barnes and Noble Books, 1998), p. 47; George Forty, *World War Two Tanks* (London: Osprey, 1995), p. 94; George Forty, *World War Two AFVs* (London: Osprey, 1996), p. 100.

27. One Rusian source claims that 3,037 SU-100s were made, or almost *eight* times as many.

28. The picture at the top of p. 129 in Peter Chamberlain and Hilary Doyle, *Encyclopedia of German Tanks of World War II* (London: Arms & Armour Press, 1999), shows a German officer standing by the side of a Jagdpanther; this gives a good idea of just how tall a vehicle it was.

29. Robert Cortese, "Jagdpanther: The Ultimate Tank Destroyer," *Military Vehicles* 77 (January–February 2000), pp. 71, 73.

30. Ian Hogg, *The Guns of World War II* (London: Macdonald and Jane's, 1976), p. 56.

31. Hans Halberstadt, *The World's Great Artillery* (London: Amber Books, 2002), p. 85.

32. In all fairness, the 88 mm was really a lousy field piece. Because the shell had to handle high velocities (it was, as mentioned, an antitank and antiaircraft weapon), it had thick walls, and proportionately less explosive filler. It also used a single cartridge; field guns use bagged powder, which means they can adjust to minimum and maximum range. Thus, a lot of the shells GIs claimed were 88s may actually have been coming from German field guns like their 105 mm cannon. Just like all German tanks became Tigers, the 88 mm had a sufficiently formidable reputation that it took on an aura of its own.

33. George Marshall, *The Winning of the War in Europe and the Pacific* (New York: Simon and Schuster, 1945), p. 97; Ian Hogg, "The 88," *War Monthly*, no. 2 (1974), p. 35.

34. Such photos—which depict German soldiers standing next to a T-35, thus giving some sense of the scale of these monsters—can be found in Steven Zaloga, Jim Kinnear, Andrey Aksenov, and Aleksander Koshchavtsev, *Stalin's Heavy Tanks* (Hong Kong: Concord Publications, 1997), bottom of p. 11; Robert Michulec, *Armor Battles on the Eastern Front (1)* (Hong Kong: Concord Publications, 1998), middle of p. 32.

35. Bryan Perrett, *German Armored Cars* (London: Osprey, 1982), p. 25; Steven Zaloga, *U.S. Light Tanks, 1944–84* (London: Osprey, 1984), p. 4.

36. Letter from General William Knowlton (ret.) to the editor, *Armor* 108 (November–December 1999), p. 3.

FURTHER READING

Baily, Charles. *Faint Praise*. Hamden, CT: Archon Books, 1983.

Bean, Tim, and Will Fowler. *Russian Tanks of World War II*. St. Paul, MN: MBI Publishing, 2002.

Bruce, Robert. *German Automatic Weapons of World War II*. London: Windrow & Greene, 1996.

Canfield, Bruce. *U.S. Infantry Arms of World War II*. Lincoln, RI: Andrew Mowbray Publications, 1994.

Chamberlain, Peter, and Hilary Doyle. *Encyclopedia of German Tanks of World War II*. London: Arms and Armour Press, 1999.

Chamberlain, Peter, and Chris Ellis. *British and American Tanks of World War II*. London: Cassell & Co., 1969.

———. *Tanks of the World*. London: Cassell & Co., 1972.

Chant, Christopher. *The World Encyclopedia of the Tank*. Somerset, UK: Patrick Stephens, 1994.

Cooper, Belton. *Death Traps*. Navato, CA: Presidio Press, 1998.

Crow, Duncan, and Robert Icks. *Encyclopedia of Armoured Cars and Half-Tracks*. London: Barrie and Jenkins, 1976.

Ezell, Edward. *Handguns of the World*. Harrisburg, PA: Stackpole Books, 1981.

———. *Small Arms of the World*. Harrisburg, PA: Stackpole Books, 1983.

Fleischer, Wolfgang. *Russian Tanks and Armored Vehicles, 1917–1945*. Atglen, PA: Schiffer Military History, 1999.

Fletcher, David, ed. *Tiger!* London: Her Majesty's Stationary Office, 1986.

Ford, Roger. *The Sherman Tank*. Osceola, WI: MBI Publishing, 1999.

———. *The Tiger Tank*. Osceola, WI: Motorbooks International, 1998.

Forty, George. *German Tanks of World War II "In Action."* London: Blandford Press, 1987.

———. *World War II Tanks*. London: Osprey, 1995.

Frankel, Nat, and Larry Smith. *Patton's Best*. New York: Hawthorne Books, 1978.

Gander, Terry. *Allied Infantry Weapons of World War II*. Marlborough: Crowood Press, 2000.

———. *The Bazooka*. London: PRC Publishing, 1998.

———. *The Browning M2*. London: PRC Publishing, 1999.

Halberstadt, Hans. *Inside the Great Tanks*. London: Windrow & Greene, 1997.

Hart, S., and R. Hart. *German Tanks of World War II*. Staplehurst: Spellmount, 1998.

Hogg, Ian. *Allied Armour of World War II*. Remsbury, UK: Crowood Press, 2000.

———. *The Complete Handgun*. New York: Exeter Books, 1979.

———. *The Complete Machine-Gun*. New York: Exeter Books, 1979.

———. *Encyclopedia of Infantry Weapons of World War II*. New York: Bison Books, 1977.

Hogg, Ian, and John Weeks, *Military Small Arms of the Twentieth Century*. Iola, WI: Krause Publications, 2000.

Hughes, Matthew, and Chris Mann. *The Panther Tank*. Osceola, WI: MBI Publishing, 2000.

———. *The T-34 Russian Battle Tank*. Osceola, WI: MBI Publishing, 1999.

Jentz, Thomas. *Germany's Panther Tank*. Atglen, PA: Schiffer Military History, 1995.

Milsom, John. *Russian Tanks, 1900–1970*. Harrisburg, PA: Stackpole Books, 1971.

Mullin, Timothy. *The Fighting Submachine Gun*, Machine Pistol, and Shotgun. Boulder, CO: Paladin Press, 1997.

———. *The 100 Greatest Combat Pistols*. Boulder, CO: Paladin Press, 1994.

———. *Testing the War Weapons*. Boulder, CO: Paladin Press, 1997.

Speilberger, Walter. *Panther & Its Variants*. Atglen, PA: Schiffer Military History, 1993.

Weeks, John. *World War II Small Arms*. London: Orbis Books, 1979.

INDEX